Publishing Division

www.EnhancedDNAPublishing.com
DenolaBurton@EnhancedDNA1.com
317-537-1438

The School Leadership Planner
An Annual Planner for School Leaders
Copyright 2022 Dr. Kenneth D. Davis
ISBN: 978-1-7369080-8-2

Printed in the United States of America

JULY

MON
LEGS

Stretching and warm-up
25 Squats
25 Sumo Squats
Repeat above March in place for 20 sec
Stretch muscles
Relax

TUES
ABS

Stretching and warm-up
20 Standing Oblique Twists
30-second Floor Plank
Repeat above
March in place for 20 seconds
Stretch muscles
Relax

WED
ARMS

Stretching and warm-up
25 Push-ups
20 Wall Tricep Pushes
Repeat above
March in place for 20 seconds
Stretch muscles
Relax

THURS
CARDIO

Stretching and warm-up
50 Jumping Jacks
30-second Sprint in place
Repeat above
March in place for 20 seconds
Stretch muscles
Relax

FRI
COMBO

Stretching and warm-up
10 Squats & 10 Sumo Squats
10 Standing Oblique Twists
March in place for 20 seconds
20 Push-ups
25 Jumping Jacks
March in place for 20 seconds
Stretch muscles
Relax

SAT
YOUR PICK

Choose from Day 1-4
to work on your chosen area:
Legs
Abs
Arms or
Cardio

SUN
REST

Take a break!
You deserve it.

workout log

Week

Date: _____ Time: _____ Week: _____

Workout Day: ① ② ③ ④ ⑤ ⑥ ⑦

Exercise	Reps	Set-1	Set-2	Set-3	Set-4	Set-5

Date: _____ Time: _____ Week: _____

Workout Day: ① ② ③ ④ ⑤ ⑥ ⑦

Exercise	Reps	Set-1	Set-2	Set-3	Set-4	Set-5

Weight

Body Fat

Chest

Right Arm

Left Arm

Waist

Hips

Right Leg

Left Leg

MY ANNUAL GOALS

PROFESSIONAL/CAMPUS GOALS

PERSONAL/GROWTH GOALS

MY REFLECTIONS: AM I ON TARGET WITH MY PROFESSIONAL GOALS? NEXT STEPS

MY REFLECTIONS: AM I ON TARGET WITH MY PERSONAL GOALS? NEXT STEPS

WHAT PROFESSIONAL DEVELOPMENT DO I NEED?

WHAT SUPPORTS DO I NEED FOR PERSONAL GROWTH?

The only person who is educated is the one who has learned how to learn and change.

Carl Rogers

MY ANNUAL GOALS

PROFESSIONAL/CAMPUS GOALS

PERSONAL/GROWTH GOALS

MY REFLECTIONS: AM I ON TARGET WITH MY PROFESSIONAL GOALS? NEXT STEPS

MY REFLECTIONS: AM I ON TARGET WITH MY PERSONAL GOALS? NEXT STEPS

WHAT PROFESSIONAL DEVELOPMENT DO I NEED?

WHAT SUPPORTS DO I NEED FOR PERSONAL GROWTH?

The only person who is educated is the one who has learned how to learn and change.
Carl Rogers

MY ANNUAL GOALS

PROFESSIONAL/CAMPUS GOALS　　　　　**PERSONAL/GROWTH GOALS**

MY REFLECTIONS: AM I ON TARGET WITH MY PROFESSIONAL GOALS? NEXT STEPS

_____

_____

_____

_____

_____

_____

MY REFLECTIONS: AM I ON TARGET WITH MY PERSONAL GOALS? NEXT STEPS

_____

_____

_____

_____

_____

_____

WHAT PROFESSIONAL DEVELOPMENT DO I NEED?

_____

_____

_____

_____

_____

_____

_____

WHAT SUPPORTS DO I NEED FOR PERSONAL GROWTH?

_____

_____

_____

_____

_____

_____

_____

The only person who is educated is the one who has learned how to learn and change.

Carl Rogers

MONTHLY PLANNER
MONTH: _____

MONDAY	TUESDAY	WEDNESDAY	THURSDAY	FRIDAY	SATURDAY	SUNDAY

PRIORITY

THIS MONTH'S LIST

Month: July Year: _____

Potential Items To Plan/Schedule:
District Board Mtg
District Principal Mtg
Plan & Schedule Vertical Team Mtg
Schedule Retention Conference w/Parents
Schedule LPACS/ELLs/ARDs
Schedule/Plan Progress Reports/Report Cards
Master Schedule Review
Schedule Team Leader/Dept Chair Mtg
Schedule Campus Admin Mtg
Schedule PLC by Level Mtg
Athletic Event Admin Coverage Schedule
Teachers I need to meet with (observe/walkthrough)

Potential Assessments:
Middle School Fluency Assessment
Renaissance 360 Grades 1-8/Alg1/Eng I/II
Benchmark/Running Records Grades 1-3 & 4-5 Recommended
Kindergarten Math & Reading Assessment
HB4545 Screener
State Level Practice Assessment by Grade by Level
English Language Development Assessment Progress Monitoring
Circle Assessment Pre-K
Credit By Exam Opportunity

Additions:
Shared Decision Making Council (SDMC) Mtg
Summer Promotion & Graduation Planning
Summer School Wrap-up for Fall Programming
Promotion/Retention Conferences

_____

_____

_____

_____

Daily Planner

Date: _____

To do

Morning _____

_____
_____
_____
_____
_____
_____

Afternoon _____

_____
_____
_____
_____
_____
_____

Evening _____

_____
_____
_____
_____
_____
_____

Goals

_____
_____
_____
_____
_____

Appointments

_____
_____

Call / Email

_____
_____

Meal Planner

_____
_____

Water Intake

◯ ◯ ◯ ◯
◯ ◯ ◯ ◯

Steps _____

Notes
If your actions inspire others to dream more, learn more, do more and become more, you are a leader.
John Quincy Adams

_____
_____
_____
_____
_____
_____

Daily Planner

Date: _____

To do

Morning _____
_____
_____
_____
_____
_____
_____
_____

Afternoon _____
_____
_____
_____
_____
_____
_____
_____

Evening _____
_____
_____
_____
_____
_____
_____

Goals
_____
_____
_____
_____

Appointments
_____
_____

Call / Email
_____
_____

Meal Planner
_____
_____

Water Intake
◯ ◯ ◯ ◯
◯ ◯ ◯ ◯

Steps _____

Notes
If your actions inspire others to dream more, learn more, do more and become more, you are a leader.
John Quincy Adams
_____
_____
_____
_____
_____
_____
_____

Date: _____

To do

Morning _____
_____
_____
_____
_____
_____
_____
_____

Afternoon _____
_____
_____
_____
_____
_____
_____

Evening _____
_____
_____
_____
_____
_____
_____

Goals
_____
_____
_____
_____
_____
_____

Appointments
_____
_____

Call / Email
_____
_____

Meal Planner
_____
_____

Water Intake
◯ ◯ ◯ ◯
◯ ◯ ◯ ◯

Steps _____

Notes
Leadership is the capacity to translate vision into reality. Warren G. Bennis
_____
_____
_____
_____
_____
_____
_____

Date: _____

To do

Morning _____
_____
_____
_____
_____
_____
_____
_____

Afternoon _____
_____
_____
_____
_____
_____
_____

Evening _____
_____
_____
_____
_____
_____
_____
_____

Goals
_____
_____
_____
_____
_____

Appointments
_____
_____
_____

Call / Email
_____
_____
_____

Meal Planner
_____
_____
_____

Water Intake
○ ○ ○ ○
○ ○ ○ ○

Steps _____

Notes
Leadership is the capacity to translate vision into reality. Warren G. Bennis
_____
_____
_____
_____
_____
_____
_____

Daily Planner

Date: _____

To do
_____

Morning _____

_____

_____

_____

_____

_____

_____

_____

Afternoon _____

_____

_____

_____

_____

_____

_____

Evening _____

_____

_____

_____

_____

_____

_____

_____

Goals
_____

_____

_____

_____

_____

_____

Appointments
_____

_____

_____

Call / Email
_____

_____

_____

Meal Planner
_____

_____

_____

Water Intake
○ ○ ○
○ ○ ○

Steps _____

Notes
Leadership is the capacity to translate vision into reality. Warren G. Bennis

_____

_____

_____

_____

_____

_____

_____

MY MEETING NOTES

MEETING NAME & DATE -

ATTENDEES -

NEXT STEPS / DEADLINES -

MEETING NOTES -

_____

_____

_____

_____

_____

_____

_____

_____

_____

_____

_____

_____

_____

_____

_____

_____

_____

_____

The purpose of education is to replace an empty mind with an open one.
Malcolm Forbes

MY MEETING NOTES

MEETING NAME & DATE -

ATTENDEES -

NEXT STEPS / DEADLINES -

MEETING NOTES -

The purpose of education is to replace an empty mind with an open one.
Malcolm Forbes

MY MEETING NOTES

MEETING NAME & DATE -

ATTENDEES -

NEXT STEPS / DEADLINES -

MEETING NOTES -

The purpose of education is to replace an empty mind with an open one.
Malcolm Forbes

MONTHLY REVIEW

MONTH OF

THIS MONTH I ACHIEVED

_____

_____

_____

_____

_____

_____

_____

_____

_____

WHAT WORKED

_____

_____

_____

WHAT DIDN'T WORK

_____

_____

_____

DO MORE OF	DO LESS OF

AUGUST

THIS MONTH'S LIST

Month: August Year: _____

Potential Items To Plan/Schedule:

District Board Mtg
District Principal Mtg
Plan & Schedule Vertical Team Mtg
Schedule Retention Conference w/Parents
Schedule LPACS/ELLs/ARDs
Schedule/Plan Progress Reports/Report Cards
Master Schedule Review for Fall
Schedule Team Leader/Dept Chair Mtg
Schedule Campus Admin Mtg
Schedule PLC by Level Mtg
Athletic Event Admin Coverage Schedule
Teachers I need to meet with (observe/walkthrough)

Potential Assessments:

Middle School Fluency Assessment
Renaissance 360 Grades 1-8/Alg1/Eng I/II
Benchmark/Running Records Grades 1-3 & 4-5 Recommended
Kindergarten Math & Reading Assessment
HB4545 Screener

Additions:

Summer Graduation Planning
Summer School Closing Routines & Data Digs
Promotion/Retention Grade Placement Comm. Mtg
Shared Decision Making Council (SDMC) Mtg

_____

_____

_____

_____

_____

_____

_____

MONTHLY PLANNER
MONTH: _____

MONDAY	TUESDAY	WEDNESDAY	THURSDAY	FRIDAY	SATURDAY	SUNDAY

PRIORITY

Daily Planner

Date: _____

To do

Morning _____

_____

_____

_____

_____

_____

_____

_____

Afternoon _____

_____

_____

_____

_____

_____

_____

_____

Evening _____

_____

_____

_____

_____

_____

_____

Goals

_____

_____

_____

_____

_____

Appointments

_____

_____

Call / Email

_____

_____

Meal Planner

_____

_____

Water Intake

◯ ◯ ◯ ◯
◯ ◯ ◯ ◯

Steps _____

Notes

The real role of leadership in education...is not and should not be command and control. The real role of leadership is climate control, creating a climate of possibility. Ken Robinson

_____

_____

_____

_____

_____

_____

Daily Planner

Date: _____

To do

Morning _____

_____

_____

_____

_____

_____

_____

_____

Afternoon _____

_____

_____

_____

_____

_____

_____

Evening _____

_____

_____

_____

_____

_____

_____

Goals

_____

_____

_____

_____

Appointments

_____

_____

Call / Email

_____

_____

Meal Planner

_____

_____

Water Intake

◯ ◯ ◯
◯ ◯ ◯

Steps _____

Notes

To improve is to change; to be perfect is to change often. Winston Churchill

_____

_____

_____

_____

_____

_____

Daily Planner

Date: _____

To do

Morning _____
_____
_____
_____
_____
_____
_____
_____
_____

Afternoon _____
_____
_____
_____
_____
_____
_____
_____

Evening _____
_____
_____
_____
_____
_____
_____
_____
_____

Goals

_____
_____
_____
_____
_____

Appointments

_____
_____
_____

Call / Email

_____
_____
_____

Meal Planner

_____
_____

Water Intake

◯ ◯ ◯
◯ ◯ ◯

Steps _____

Notes

He who has never learned to obey cannot be a good commander. Aristotle

_____
_____
_____
_____
_____
_____
_____

Daily Planner

Date: _____

To do

Morning _____

_____

_____

_____

_____

_____

_____

_____

Afternoon _____

_____

_____

_____

_____

_____

_____

Evening _____

_____

_____

_____

_____

_____

_____

Goals

_____

_____

_____

_____

Appointments

_____

_____

Call / Email

_____

_____

Meal Planner

_____

_____

Water Intake

◯ ◯ ◯ ◯
◯ ◯ ◯ ◯

Steps _____

Notes

Before you are a leader, success is all about yourself. When you become a leader, success is all about growing others. Jack Welch

_____

_____

_____

_____

_____

_____

_____

Daily Planner

Date: _____

To do

Morning _____

_____

_____

_____

_____

_____

_____

_____

Afternoon _____

_____

_____

_____

_____

_____

_____

Evening _____

_____

_____

_____

_____

_____

_____

_____

Goals

_____

_____

_____

_____

_____

Appointments

_____

_____

Call / Email

_____

_____

Meal Planner

_____

_____

Water Intake

◯ ◯ ◯ ◯
◯ ◯ ◯ ◯

Steps _____

Notes

Before you are a leader, success is all about yourself. When you become a leader, success is all about growing others. Jack Welch

_____

_____

_____

_____

_____

_____

_____

MY MEETING NOTES

MEETING NAME & DATE -

ATTENDEES -

NEXT STEPS / DEADLINES -

MEETING NOTES -

_____

_____

_____

_____

_____

_____

_____

_____

_____

_____

_____

_____

_____

_____

_____

_____

_____

The only person who is educated is the one who has learned how to learn and change.
Carl Rogers

MY MEETING NOTES

MEETING NAME & DATE -

ATTENDEES -

NEXT STEPS / DEADLINES -

MEETING NOTES -

The only person who is educated is the one who has learned how to learn and change.
Carl Rogers

SEPTEMBER

THIS MONTH'S LIST

Month: September Year: _____

Potential Items To Plan/Schedule:
District Board Mtg
District Principal Mtg
Plan & Schedule Vertical Team Mtg
Schedule Retention Conference w/Parents
Schedule LPACS/ELLs/ARDs
Schedule/Plan Progress Reports/Report Cards
Master Schedule Review
Schedule Team Leader/Dept Chair Mtg
Schedule Campus Admin Mtg
Schedule PLC by Level Mtg
Athletic Event Admin Coverage Schedule
Teachers I need to meet with (observe/walkthrough)

Potential Assessments:
Middle School Fluency Assessment
Renaissance 360 Grades 1-8/Alg1/Eng I/II
Benchmark/Running Records Grades 1-3 & 4-5 Recommended
Kindergarten Math & Reading Assessment
HB4545 Screener
State Level Practice Assessment by Grade by Level
English Language Development Assessment Progress
Monitoring
Circle Assessment Pre-K
Credit By Exam Opportunity

Additions:
Shared Decision Making Council (SDMC) Mtg

_____
_____
_____
_____

MONTHLY PLANNER
MONTH: _____

MONDAY	TUESDAY	WEDNESDAY	THURSDAY	FRIDAY	SATURDAY	SUNDAY

PRIORITY

To Do List This Week

Day _____

Date & Month _____

No.	To Do	Yes/No
		☐ ☐
		☐ ☐
		☐ ☐
		☐ ☐
		☐ ☐
		☐ ☐
		☐ ☐
		☐ ☐
		☐ ☐
		☐ ☐
		☐ ☐
		☐ ☐
		☐ ☐
		☐ ☐
		☐ ☐
		☐ ☐
		☐ ☐
		☐ ☐
		☐ ☐
		☐ ☐

Notes _____
_____
_____
_____

Daily Planner

Date: _____

To do

Morning _____
_____
_____
_____
_____
_____
_____
_____

Afternoon _____
_____
_____
_____
_____
_____
_____
_____

Evening _____
_____
_____
_____
_____
_____
_____
_____

Goals
_____
_____
_____
_____

Appointments
_____
_____

Call / Email
_____
_____

Meal Planner
_____
_____

Water Intake
○ ○ ○
○ ○ ○

Steps _____

Notes

Education is the most powerful weapon which you can use to change the world. Nelson Mandela

_____
_____
_____
_____
_____
_____

Daily Planner

Date: _____

To do

Morning _____

_____
_____
_____
_____
_____
_____
_____
_____

Afternoon _____

_____
_____
_____
_____
_____
_____
_____

Evening _____

_____
_____
_____
_____
_____
_____
_____

Goals

_____
_____
_____
_____
_____

Appointments

_____
_____

Call / Email

_____
_____

Meal Planner

_____
_____

Water Intake

◯ ◯ ◯ ◯
◯ ◯ ◯ ◯

Steps _____

Notes

**Education is the most powerful weapon which
you can use to change the world.
Nelson Mandela**

_____
_____
_____
_____
_____
_____
_____

Daily Planner

Date: _____

To do

Morning _____

_____

_____

_____

_____

_____

_____

_____

Afternoon _____

_____

_____

_____

_____

_____

_____

_____

Evening _____

_____

_____

_____

_____

_____

_____

_____

Goals

_____

_____

_____

_____

Appointments

_____

_____

Call / Email

_____

_____

Meal Planner

_____

_____

Water Intake

◯ ◯ ◯ ◯
◯ ◯ ◯ ◯

Steps _____

Notes

I am always ready to learn although I do
not always like being taught.
Winston Churchill

_____

_____

_____

_____

_____

_____

_____

Daily Planner

Date: _____

To do

Morning _____

_____

_____

_____

_____

_____

_____

Afternoon _____

_____

_____

_____

_____

_____

_____

Evening _____

_____

_____

_____

_____

_____

_____

Goals

_____

_____

_____

_____

Appointments

_____

_____

Call / Email

_____

_____

Meal Planner

_____

_____

Water Intake

◯ ◯ ◯ ◯
◯ ◯ ◯ ◯

Steps _____

Notes

Never let formal education get in the way of your learning. Mark Twain

_____

_____

_____

_____

_____

_____

_____

Daily Planner

Date: _____

To do

Morning _____

_____

_____

_____

_____

_____

_____

_____

Afternoon _____

_____

_____

_____

_____

_____

_____

_____

Evening _____

_____

_____

_____

_____

_____

_____

Goals

_____

_____

_____

_____

Appointments

_____

_____

Call / Email

_____

_____

Meal Planner

_____

_____

Water Intake

◯ ◯ ◯ ◯
◯ ◯ ◯ ◯

Steps _____

Notes

A man's mind, stretched by new ideas, may never return to its original dimensions. Oliver Wendell Holmes Jr.

_____

_____

_____

_____

_____

_____

_____

Daily Planner

Date: _____

To do

Morning _____

_____

_____

_____

_____

_____

_____

_____

Afternoon _____

_____

_____

_____

_____

_____

_____

Evening _____

_____

_____

_____

_____

_____

Goals

_____

_____

_____

_____

Appointments

_____

_____

Call / Email

_____

_____

Meal Planner

_____

_____

Water Intake

○ ○ ○
○ ○ ○

Steps _____

Notes

**Leadership and learning are indispensable
to each other. John F. Kennedy**

_____

_____

_____

_____

_____

_____

_____

Daily Planner

Date: _____

To do

Morning _____

_____

_____

_____

_____

_____

_____

_____

Afternoon _____

_____

_____

_____

_____

_____

_____

Evening _____

_____

_____

_____

_____

_____

_____

Goals

_____

_____

_____

_____

_____

Appointments

_____

_____

Call / Email

_____

_____

Meal Planner

_____

_____

Water Intake

◯ ◯ ◯ ◯
◯ ◯ ◯ ◯

Steps _____

Notes

Through education comes understanding. Through understanding comes true appreciation. All children are artists. The problem is how to remain an artist once he grows up. - Pablo Picasso

_____

_____

_____

_____

_____

workout log

Week

Date : _____ Time : _____ Week : _____

Weight

Workout Day : ① ② ③ ④ ⑤ ⑥ ⑦

Body Fat

Exercise	Reps	Set -1	Set -2	Set -3	Set -4	Set -5

Chest

Right Arm

Left Arm

Date : _____ Time : _____ Week : _____

Waist

Workout Day : ① ② ③ ④ ⑤ ⑥ ⑦

Hips

Exercise	Reps	Set -1	Set -2	Set -3	Set -4	Set -5

Right Leg

Left Leg

To Do List This Week

Day _____

Date & Month _____

No.	To Do	Yes/No
_____	_____	☐ ☐
_____	_____	☐ ☐
_____	_____	☐ ☐
_____	_____	☐ ☐
_____	_____	☐ ☐
_____	_____	☐ ☐
_____	_____	☐ ☐
_____	_____	☐ ☐
_____	_____	☐ ☐
_____	_____	☐ ☐
_____	_____	☐ ☐
_____	_____	☐ ☐
_____	_____	☐ ☐
_____	_____	☐ ☐
_____	_____	☐ ☐
_____	_____	☐ ☐
_____	_____	☐ ☐
_____	_____	☐ ☐
_____	_____	☐ ☐

Notes _____

_____

_____

_____

Daily Planner

Date: _____

To do

Morning _____

_____

_____

_____

_____

_____

_____

_____

Afternoon _____

_____

_____

_____

_____

_____

_____

_____

Evening _____

_____

_____

_____

_____

_____

_____

Goals

_____

_____

_____

_____

_____

Appointments

_____

_____

Call / Email

_____

_____

Meal Planner

_____

_____

Water Intake

◯ ◯ ◯ ◯
◯ ◯ ◯ ◯

Steps _____

Notes

A master can tell you what he expects of you. A teacher, though, awakens your own expectations.
Patricia Neal

_____

_____

_____

_____

_____

_____

_____

Daily Planner

Date: _____

To do

Morning _____
_____
_____
_____
_____
_____
_____
_____

Afternoon _____
_____
_____
_____
_____
_____
_____
_____

Evening _____
_____
_____
_____
_____
_____
_____
_____

Goals
_____
_____
_____
_____
_____

Appointments
_____
_____
_____

Call / Email
_____
_____
_____

Meal Planner
_____
_____
_____

Water Intake
○ ○ ○ ○
○ ○ ○ ○

Steps _____

Notes
Our schools have a doubly hard task, not just improving reading, writing and arithmetic but entrepreneurship, innovation, and creativity.
Ken Robinson
_____
_____
_____
_____
_____
_____
_____

Daily Planner

Date: _____

To do

Morning _____
_____
_____
_____
_____
_____
_____
_____

Afternoon _____
_____
_____
_____
_____
_____
_____

Evening _____
_____
_____
_____
_____
_____
_____

Goals

_____
_____
_____
_____

Appointments

_____
_____

Call / Email

_____
_____

Meal Planner

_____
_____

Water Intake

◯ ◯ ◯
◯ ◯ ◯

Steps _____

Notes

Don't limit a child to your own learning, for he was born in another time. Rabbinical Saying

_____
_____
_____
_____
_____
_____
_____
_____

Daily Planner

Date: _____

To do

Morning _____
_____
_____
_____
_____
_____
_____

Afternoon _____
_____
_____
_____
_____
_____

Evening _____
_____
_____
_____
_____
_____
_____
_____

Goals
_____
_____
_____
_____
_____

Appointments
_____
_____

Call / Email
_____
_____

Meal Planner
_____
_____

Water Intake
◯ ◯ ◯ ◯
◯ ◯ ◯ ◯

Steps _____

Notes

"It is not about the technology; it's about sharing knowledge and information, communicating efficiently, building learning communities and creating a culture of professionalism in schools. These are the key responsibilities of all educational leaders". Marion Ginapolis

_____
_____
_____
_____
_____

Daily Planner

Date: _____

To do

Morning _____
_____
_____
_____
_____
_____
_____

Afternoon _____
_____
_____
_____
_____
_____
_____

Evening _____
_____
_____
_____
_____
_____
_____
_____
_____

Goals

_____
_____
_____
_____

Appointments

_____
_____

Call / Email

_____
_____

Meal Planner

_____
_____

Water Intake

◯ ◯ ◯ ◯
◯ ◯ ◯ ◯

Steps _____

Notes

If the education and studies of children were suited to their inclinations and capacities, many would be made useful members of society that otherwise would make no figure in it. Samuel Richardson

_____
_____
_____
_____

Daily Planner

Date: _____

To do

Morning _____
_____
_____
_____
_____
_____
_____
_____

Afternoon _____
_____
_____
_____
_____
_____
_____

Evening _____
_____
_____
_____
_____
_____
_____

Goals
_____
_____
_____
_____
_____

Appointments
_____
_____

Call / Email
_____
_____

Meal Planner
_____
_____

Water Intake
○ ○ ○
○ ○ ○

Steps _____

Notes

I cannot teach anybody anything, I can only make them think. Socrates

_____
_____
_____
_____
_____
_____

Daily Planner

Date: _____

To do

Morning _____

_____
_____
_____
_____
_____
_____
_____

Afternoon _____

_____
_____
_____
_____
_____
_____
_____

Evening _____

_____
_____
_____
_____
_____
_____
_____

Goals

_____
_____
_____
_____
_____
_____

Appointments

_____
_____
_____

Call / Email

_____
_____

Meal Planner

_____
_____
_____

Water Intake

◯ ◯ ◯ ◯
◯ ◯ ◯ ◯

Steps _____

Notes

One learns by doing a thing; for though you think
you know it, you have no certainty until you try.
Sophocles

_____
_____
_____
_____
_____
_____
_____
_____

workout log

Week

Date :   Time :   Week :

Workout Day : ① ② ③ ④ ⑤ ⑥ ⑦

Exercise	Reps	Set -1	Set -2	Set -3	Set -4	Set -5

Date :   Time :   Week :

Workout Day : ① ② ③ ④ ⑤ ⑥ ⑦

Exercise	Reps	Set -1	Set -2	Set -3	Set -4	Set -5

Weight

Body Fat

Chest

Right Arm

Left Arm

Waist

Hips

Right Leg

Left Leg

To Do List This Week

Day _____

Date & Month _____

No.	To Do	Yes/No	
___	_____	☐	☐
___	_____	☐	☐
___	_____	☐	☐
___	_____	☐	☐
___	_____	☐	☐
___	_____	☐	☐
___	_____	☐	☐
___	_____	☐	☐
___	_____	☐	☐
___	_____	☐	☐
___	_____	☐	☐
___	_____	☐	☐
___	_____	☐	☐
___	_____	☐	☐
___	_____	☐	☐
___	_____	☐	☐
___	_____	☐	☐
___	_____	☐	☐
___	_____	☐	☐
___	_____	☐	☐

Notes _____
_____
_____
_____

Daily Planner

Date: _____

To do

Morning _____

_____

_____

_____

_____

_____

_____

_____

Afternoon _____

_____

_____

_____

_____

_____

_____

Evening _____

_____

_____

_____

_____

_____

_____

Goals

_____

_____

_____

_____

_____

Appointments

_____

_____

_____

Call / Email

_____

_____

_____

Meal Planner

_____

_____

_____

Water Intake

◯ ◯ ◯ ◯
◯ ◯ ◯ ◯

Steps _____

Notes

A teacher is one who makes himself progressively unnecessary. Thomas Carruthers

_____

_____

_____

_____

_____

_____

Daily Planner

Date: _____

To do

Morning _____

_____

_____

_____

_____

_____

_____

_____

Afternoon _____

_____

_____

_____

_____

_____

_____

Evening _____

_____

_____

_____

_____

_____

_____

Goals

_____

_____

_____

_____

_____

Appointments

_____

_____

_____

Call / Email

_____

_____

Meal Planner

_____

_____

Water Intake

○ ○ ○

○ ○ ○

Steps _____

Notes

An education isn't how much you have committed to memory, or even how much you know. It's being able to differentiate between what you do know and what you don't. It's knowing where to go to find out what you need to know; and it's knowing how to use the information you get. William Feather

_____

_____

_____

_____

_____

Daily Planner

Date: _____

To do

Morning _____
_____
_____
_____
_____
_____
_____
_____

Afternoon _____
_____
_____
_____
_____
_____
_____
_____

Evening _____
_____
_____
_____
_____
_____
_____
_____

Goals

_____
_____
_____
_____
_____
_____

Appointments

_____
_____
_____

Call / Email

_____
_____
_____

Meal Planner

_____
_____
_____

Water Intake

○ ○ ○ ○
○ ○ ○ ○

Steps _____

Notes

The rule for every man is, not to depend on the education which other men have prepared for him —not even to consent to it; but to strive to see things as they are, and to be himself as he is. Defeat lies in self-surrender. Woodrow Wilson

_____
_____
_____
_____
_____

Daily Planner

Date: _____

To do

Morning _____
_____
_____
_____
_____
_____
_____
_____

Afternoon _____
_____
_____
_____
_____
_____
_____

Evening _____
_____
_____
_____
_____
_____
_____
_____

Goals
_____
_____
_____
_____
_____

Appointments
_____
_____
_____

Call / Email
_____
_____

Meal Planner
_____
_____

Water Intake
○ ○ ○ ○
○ ○ ○ ○

Steps _____

Notes
Tell me and I forget, teach me and I may remember,
involve me and I learn. Benjamin Franklin
_____
_____
_____
_____
_____
_____
_____

Daily Planner

Date: _____

To do

Morning _____
_____
_____
_____
_____
_____
_____
_____

Afternoon _____
_____
_____
_____
_____
_____
_____

Evening _____
_____
_____
_____
_____
_____
_____

Goals
_____
_____
_____
_____
_____

Appointments
_____
_____

Call / Email
_____
_____

Meal Planner
_____
_____

Water Intake
◯ ◯ ◯ ◯
◯ ◯ ◯ ◯

Steps _____

Notes
I am not a teacher, but an awakener.
Robert Frost
_____
_____
_____
_____
_____
_____

Daily Planner

Date: _____

To do

Morning _____

_____

_____

_____

_____

_____

_____

_____

Afternoon _____

_____

_____

_____

_____

_____

_____

_____

Evening _____

_____

_____

_____

_____

_____

_____

_____

Goals

_____

_____

_____

_____

_____

_____

Appointments

_____

_____

_____

Call / Email

_____

_____

_____

Meal Planner

_____

_____

_____

Water Intake

◯ ◯ ◯ ◯
◯ ◯ ◯ ◯

Steps _____

Notes

Spoon feeding in the long run teaches us nothing but the shape of the spoon. E.M. Forster

_____

_____

_____

_____

_____

_____

_____

Daily Planner

Date: _____

To do

Morning _____

_____

_____

_____

_____

_____

_____

_____

Afternoon _____

_____

_____

_____

_____

_____

_____

Evening _____

_____

_____

_____

_____

_____

_____

_____

Goals

_____

_____

_____

_____

_____

Appointments

_____

_____

Call / Email

_____

_____

Meal Planner

_____

_____

Water Intake

◯ ◯ ◯
◯ ◯ ◯

Steps _____

Notes

'The measure of intelligence is the ability to change'
-Albert Einstein

_____

_____

_____

_____

_____

_____

workout log

Week

Date : _____ Time : _____ Week : _____

| Workout Day : | ① | ② | ③ | ④ | ⑤ | ⑥ | ⑦ |

Exercise	Reps	Set -1	Set -2	Set -3	Set -4	Set -5

Date : _____ Time : _____ Week : _____

| Workout Day : | ① | ② | ③ | ④ | ⑤ | ⑥ | ⑦ |

Exercise	Reps	Set -1	Set -2	Set -3	Set -4	Set -5

Weight

Body Fat

Chest

Right Arm

Left Arm

Waist

Hips

Right Leg

Left Leg

To Do List This Week

Day ——————

Date & Month ——————

No.	To Do	Yes/No
___	_____	☐ ☐
___	_____	☐ ☐
___	_____	☐ ☐
___	_____	☐ ☐
___	_____	☐ ☐
___	_____	☐ ☐
___	_____	☐ ☐
___	_____	☐ ☐
___	_____	☐ ☐
___	_____	☐ ☐
___	_____	☐ ☐
___	_____	☐ ☐
___	_____	☐ ☐
___	_____	☐ ☐
___	_____	☐ ☐
___	_____	☐ ☐
___	_____	☐ ☐
___	_____	☐ ☐
___	_____	☐ ☐
___	_____	☐ ☐

Notes _____

_____

_____

_____

Daily Planner

Date: _____

To do

Morning _____

_____

_____

_____

_____

_____

_____

_____

Afternoon _____

_____

_____

_____

_____

_____

_____

Evening _____

_____

_____

_____

_____

_____

_____

_____

Goals

_____

_____

_____

_____

_____

Appointments

_____

_____

Call / Email

_____

_____

Meal Planner

_____

_____

Water Intake

○ ○ ○ ○
○ ○ ○ ○

Steps _____

Notes

'The greatest discovery of all time is that a person can change his future by merely changing his attitude' -Oprah Winfrey

_____

_____

_____

_____

_____

_____

Daily Planner

Date: _____

To do

Morning _____

_____

_____

_____

_____

_____

_____

_____

Afternoon _____

_____

_____

_____

_____

_____

_____

Evening _____

_____

_____

_____

_____

_____

_____

Goals

_____

_____

_____

_____

_____

Appointments

_____

_____

Call / Email

_____

_____

Meal Planner

_____

_____

Water Intake

◯ ◯ ◯ ◯
◯ ◯ ◯ ◯

Steps _____

Notes

'Every day the clock resets. Your wins don't matter.
Your failures don't matter. Don't stress on what was,
fight for what could be.' -Sean Higgins

_____

_____

_____

_____

_____

_____

_____

Daily Planner

Date: _____

To do

Morning _____
_____
_____
_____
_____
_____
_____
_____
_____

Afternoon _____
_____
_____
_____
_____
_____
_____

Evening _____
_____
_____
_____
_____
_____
_____
_____

Goals

_____
_____
_____
_____
_____

Appointments

_____
_____

Call / Email

_____
_____

Meal Planner

_____
_____

Water Intake

◯ ◯ ◯ ◯
◯ ◯ ◯ ◯

Steps _____

Notes

'Don't let rejection create self-doubt. The founder of Starbucks was turned down by 217 of the 242 investors he initially spoke with.' -Elizabeth Galbut

_____
_____
_____
_____
_____
_____
_____

Daily Planner

Date: _____

To do

Morning _____

_____

_____

_____

_____

_____

_____

Afternoon _____

_____

_____

_____

_____

_____

_____

Evening _____

_____

_____

_____

_____

_____

_____

Goals

_____

_____

_____

_____

_____

Appointments

_____

_____

Call / Email

_____

_____

Meal Planner

_____

_____

Water Intake

○ ○ ○ ○
○ ○ ○ ○

Steps _____

Notes

'Everyone thinks of changing the world, but no one thinks of changing himself.' -Leo Tolstoy

_____

_____

_____

_____

_____

_____

_____

Daily Planner

Date: _____

To do

Morning _____
_____
_____
_____
_____
_____
_____
_____

Afternoon _____
_____
_____
_____
_____
_____
_____

Evening _____
_____
_____
_____
_____
_____
_____

Goals

_____
_____
_____
_____

Appointments

_____
_____

Call / Email

_____
_____

Meal Planner

_____
_____

Water Intake

◯ ◯ ◯ ◯
◯ ◯ ◯ ◯

Steps _____

Notes

'Play to your strengths. If you aren't great at something, do more of what you're great at.'
Jason Lemkin

_____
_____
_____
_____
_____
_____

Daily Planner

Date: _____

To do

Morning _____
_____
_____
_____
_____
_____
_____
_____

Afternoon _____
_____
_____
_____
_____
_____
_____

Evening _____
_____
_____
_____
_____
_____

Goals

_____
_____
_____
_____
_____

Appointments

_____
_____

Call / Email

_____
_____

Meal Planner

_____
_____

Water Intake

◯ ◯ ◯ ◯
◯ ◯ ◯ ◯

Steps _____

Notes

'Every great dream begins with a dreamer. Always remember, you have within you the strength, the patience, and the passion to reach for the stars to change the world.' -Harriet Tubman

_____
_____
_____
_____
_____
_____

Daily Planner

Date: _____

To do

Morning _____

_____
_____
_____
_____
_____
_____
_____

Afternoon _____

_____
_____
_____
_____
_____
_____
_____

Evening _____

_____
_____
_____
_____
_____
_____

Goals

_____
_____
_____
_____
_____

Appointments

_____
_____

Call / Email

_____
_____

Meal Planner

_____
_____

Water Intake

◯ ◯ ◯ ◯
◯ ◯ ◯ ◯

Steps _____

Notes

"To improve is to change; to be perfect is to change often." -Winston Churchill

_____
_____
_____
_____
_____
_____
_____

workout log

Week

Date: _____ Time: _____ Week: _____

Workout Day: ① ② ③ ④ ⑤ ⑥ ⑦

Exercise	Reps	Set-1	Set-2	Set-3	Set-4	Set-5

Date: _____ Time: _____ Week: _____

Workout Day: ① ② ③ ④ ⑤ ⑥ ⑦

Exercise	Reps	Set-1	Set-2	Set-3	Set-4	Set-5

Weight

Body Fat

Chest

Right Arm

Left Arm

Waist

Hips

Right Leg

Left Leg

MY MEETING NOTES

MEETING NAME & DATE -

ATTENDEES -

NEXT STEPS / DEADLINES -

MEETING NOTES -

Example is not the main thing in influencing others. It is the only thing.
Albert Schweitzer

MY MEETING NOTES

MEETING NAME & DATE -

ATTENDEES -

NEXT STEPS / DEADLINES -

MEETING NOTES -

Education is not the filling of a pail, but the lighting of a fire.
William Butler Yeats

MY MEETING NOTES

MEETING NAME & DATE -

ATTENDEES -

NEXT STEPS / DEADLINES -

MEETING NOTES -

_____
_____
_____
_____
_____
_____
_____
_____
_____
_____
_____
_____
_____
_____
_____
_____
_____
_____
_____

Education is simply the soul of a society as it passes from one generation to another.
Gilbert K. Chersterton

MY MEETING NOTES

MEETING NAME & DATE -

ATTENDEES -

NEXT STEPS / DEADLINES -

MEETING NOTES -

Our deepest fear is not that we are inadequate. Our deepest fear is that we are powerful beyond measure. It is our light, not our darkness, that most frightens us. Marianne Williamson

MY MEETING NOTES

MEETING NAME & DATE -

ATTENDEES -

NEXT STEPS / DEADLINES -

MEETING NOTES -

The object of education is to prepare the young to educate themselves throughout their lives.
Robert M. Hutchins

MY MEETING NOTES

MEETING NAME & DATE -

ATTENDEES -

NEXT STEPS / DEADLINES -

MEETING NOTES -

Never tell people how to do things. Tell them what to do and they will surprise you with their ingenuity. George S. Patton

MY MEETING NOTES

MEETING NAME & DATE -

ATTENDEES -

NEXT STEPS / DEADLINES -

MEETING NOTES -

A leader is best when people barely know he exists, when his work is done, his aim fulfilled, they will say: we did it ourselves. Laozi

MY MEETING NOTES

MEETING NAME & DATE -

ATTENDEES -

NEXT STEPS / DEADLINES -

MEETING NOTES -

It is the mark of an educated mind to be able to entertain a thought without accepting it.
Aristotle

MY MEETING NOTES

MEETING NAME & DATE -

ATTENDEES -

NEXT STEPS / DEADLINES -

MEETING NOTES -

Leadership is the art of getting someone else to do something you want done because he wants to do it. Dwight D. Eisenhower

MONTHLY REVIEW

THIS MONTH I ACHIEVED

_____

_____

_____

_____

_____

_____

_____

_____

_____

WHAT WORKED

_____

_____

_____

_____

WHAT DIDN'T WORK

_____

_____

_____

_____

DO MORE OF	DO LESS OF

MONTHLY REVIEW

MONTH OF

THIS MONTH I ACHIEVED

_____
_____
_____
_____
_____
_____
_____
_____

WHAT WORKED

_____
_____
_____
_____

WHAT DIDN'T WORK

_____
_____
_____
_____

DO MORE OF	DO LESS OF

OCTOBER

MON
LEGS

Stretching and warm-up
25 Squats
25 Sumo Squats
Repeat above March in place for 20 sec
Stretch muscles
Relax

TUES
ABS

Stretching and warm-up
20 Standing Oblique Twists
30-second Floor Plank
Repeat above
March in place for 20 seconds
Stretch muscles
Relax

WED
ARMS

Stretching and warm-up
25 Push-ups
20 Wall Tricep Pushes
Repeat above
March in place for 20 seconds
Stretch muscles
Relax

THURS
CARDIO

Stretching and warm-up
50 Jumping Jacks
30-second Sprint in place
Repeat above
March in place for 20 seconds
Stretch muscles
Relax

FRI
COMBO

Stretching and warm-up
10 Squats & 10 Sumo Squats
10 Standing Oblique Twists
March in place for 20 seconds
20 Push-ups
25 Jumping Jacks
March in place for 20 seconds
Stretch muscles
Relax

SAT
YOUR PICK

Choose from Day 1-4
to work on your chosen area:
Legs
Abs
Arms or
Cardio

SUN
REST

Take a break!
You deserve it.

workout log

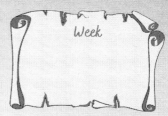

Week

Date: _____ Time: _____ Week: _____

Workout Day: ① ② ③ ④ ⑤ ⑥ ⑦

Exercise	Reps	Set -1	Set -2	Set -3	Set -4	Set -5

Date: _____ Time: _____ Week: _____

Workout Day: ① ② ③ ④ ⑤ ⑥ ⑦

Exercise	Reps	Set -1	Set -2	Set -3	Set -4	Set -5

Weight

Body Fat

Chest

Right Arm

Left Arm

Waist

Hips

Right Leg

Left Leg

THIS MONTH'S LIST
Month: October Year: _____

Potential Items to Plan/Schedule
District Board Mtg
District Principal Mtg
Campus Admin Mtg
Vertical Team Mtg
Professional Learning Community (PLC)
Parent Conferences
LPACs/ELLs/ARD Mtg
Progress Report/Report Cards
Master Schedule Review
Team Leader/Dept. Chair Mtg
Athletic Event Admin Coverage Schedule
Teachers I need to meet with (observe/walkthrough)

Potential Assessments
Middle School Fluency Assessment
Renaissance 360 Grades 1-8/Alg 1/Eng I/II
Kindergarten Math & Reading Assessment
HB4545 Screener
PSAT/SAT Assessment
District Snapshot Assessment

Additions
Shared Decision Making Council (SDMC)

_____

_____

_____

_____

_____

_____

To Do List This Week

Day _____

Date & Month _____

No.	To Do	Yes/No
_____	_____	☐ ☐
_____	_____	☐ ☐
_____	_____	☐ ☐
_____	_____	☐ ☐
_____	_____	☐ ☐
_____	_____	☐ ☐
_____	_____	☐ ☐
_____	_____	☐ ☐
_____	_____	☐ ☐
_____	_____	☐ ☐
_____	_____	☐ ☐
_____	_____	☐ ☐
_____	_____	☐ ☐
_____	_____	☐ ☐
_____	_____	☐ ☐
_____	_____	☐ ☐
_____	_____	☐ ☐
_____	_____	☐ ☐
_____	_____	☐ ☐
_____	_____	☐ ☐

Notes _____

_____

_____

_____

Daily Planner

Date: _____

To do

Morning _____
_____
_____
_____
_____
_____
_____
_____

Afternoon _____
_____
_____
_____
_____
_____
_____

Evening _____
_____
_____
_____
_____
_____
_____

Goals
_____
_____
_____
_____
_____

Appointments
_____
_____
_____

Call / Email
_____
_____
_____

Meal Planner
_____
_____

Water Intake
○ ○ ○
○ ○ ○

Steps _____

Notes

If you can dream it, you can make it so. Belva Davis
_____
_____
_____
_____
_____
_____

Daily Planner

Date: _____

To do

Morning _____

_____

_____

_____

_____

_____

Afternoon _____

_____

_____

_____

_____

Evening _____

_____

_____

_____

_____

_____

Goals

_____

_____

_____

_____

Appointments

_____

_____

Call / Email

_____

_____

Meal Planner

_____

_____

Water Intake

○ ○ ○
○ ○ ○

Steps _____

Notes

If you dream it, you can achieve it. Zig Ziglar

_____

_____

_____

_____

_____

_____

_____

Daily Planner

Date: _____

To do

Morning _____

_____

_____

_____

_____

_____

_____

_____

Afternoon _____

_____

_____

_____

_____

_____

_____

Evening _____

_____

_____

_____

_____

_____

_____

Goals

_____

_____

_____

_____

_____

Appointments

_____

_____

_____

Call / Email

_____

_____

_____

Meal Planner

_____

_____

Water Intake

◯ ◯ ◯ ◯
◯ ◯ ◯ ◯

Steps _____

Notes

If you can dream it, you can do it. Walt Disney

_____

_____

_____

_____

_____

_____

_____

Daily Planner

Date: _____

To do

Morning _____

_____

_____

_____

_____

_____

_____

_____

Afternoon _____

_____

_____

_____

_____

_____

_____

Evening _____

_____

_____

_____

_____

_____

_____

Goals

_____

_____

_____

_____

_____

Appointments

_____

_____

Call / Email

_____

_____

Meal Planner

_____

_____

Water Intake

◯ ◯ ◯
◯ ◯ ◯

Steps _____

Notes

There goes my people. I must follow them, for I am
their leader. Mahatma Gandhi

_____

_____

_____

_____

_____

_____

_____

_____

Daily Planner

Date: _____

To do

Morning _____

_____

_____

_____

_____

_____

_____

_____

Afternoon _____

_____

_____

_____

_____

_____

_____

_____

Evening _____

_____

_____

_____

_____

_____

_____

Goals

_____

_____

_____

_____

_____

Appointments

_____

_____

Call / Email

_____

_____

Meal Planner

_____

_____

Water Intake

○ ○ ○ ○
○ ○ ○ ○

Steps _____

Notes

No man is good enough to govern another man
without the other's consent. Abraham Lincoln

_____

_____

_____

_____

_____

_____

_____

Daily Planner

Date: _____

To do

Morning _____

_____

_____

_____

_____

_____

_____

_____

Afternoon _____

_____

_____

_____

_____

_____

_____

_____

Evening _____

_____

_____

_____

_____

_____

_____

_____

Goals

_____

_____

_____

_____

_____

Appointments

_____

_____

_____

Call / Email

_____

_____

_____

Meal Planner

_____

_____

Water Intake

○ ○ ○ ○
○ ○ ○ ○

Steps _____

Notes

**He who has learned how to obey will know
how to command. Solon**

_____

_____

_____

_____

_____

_____

_____

Daily Planner

Date: _____

To do

Morning _____

_____

_____

_____

_____

_____

_____

Afternoon _____

_____

_____

_____

_____

_____

_____

Evening _____

_____

_____

_____

_____

_____

_____

Goals

_____

_____

_____

_____

_____

Appointments

_____

_____

Call / Email

_____

_____

Meal Planner

_____

_____

Water Intake

◯ ◯ ◯ ◯
◯ ◯ ◯ ◯

Steps _____

Notes

The first responsibility of a leader is to define reality. Max De Pree

_____

_____

_____

_____

_____

_____

workout log

Week

Date: [   ] Time: [   ] Week: [   ]

Workout Day: ① ② ③ ④ ⑤ ⑥ ⑦

Exercise	Reps	Set -1	Set -2	Set -3	Set -4	Set -5

Date: [   ] Time: [   ] Week: [   ]

Workout Day: ① ② ③ ④ ⑤ ⑥ ⑦

Exercise	Reps	Set -1	Set -2	Set -3	Set -4	Set -5

Weight

Body Fat

Chest

Right Arm

Left Arm

Waist

Hips

Right Leg

Left Leg

To Do List This Week

Day ——————

Date & Month ——————

No.	To Do	Yes/No
		☐ ☐
		☐ ☐
		☐ ☐
		☐ ☐
		☐ ☐
		☐ ☐
		☐ ☐
		☐ ☐
		☐ ☐
		☐ ☐
		☐ ☐
		☐ ☐
		☐ ☐
		☐ ☐
		☐ ☐
		☐ ☐
		☐ ☐
		☐ ☐
		☐ ☐
		☐ ☐

Notes ——————————————————————

——————————————————————————

——————————————————————————

——————————————————————————

Daily Planner

Date: _____

To do

Morning _____
_____
_____
_____
_____
_____
_____
_____

Afternoon _____
_____
_____
_____
_____
_____
_____
_____

Evening _____
_____
_____
_____
_____
_____
_____

Goals
_____
_____
_____
_____
_____
_____

Appointments
_____
_____
_____

Call / Email
_____
_____
_____

Meal Planner
_____
_____
_____

Water Intake
○ ○ ○ ○
○ ○ ○ ○

Steps _____

Notes
Leaders aren't born, they are made. Vince Lombardi
_____
_____
_____
_____
_____
_____
_____

Date: _____

To do

Morning _____

_____

_____

_____

_____

_____

_____

Afternoon _____

_____

_____

_____

_____

_____

Evening _____

_____

_____

_____

_____

_____

_____

Goals

_____

_____

_____

_____

Appointments

_____

_____

Call / Email

_____

_____

Meal Planner

_____

_____

Water Intake

Steps _____

Notes

No general can fight his battles alone. He must
depend upon his lieutenants, and his success
depends upon his reality to select the right man
for the right place.
Phillip Danforth Armor

_____

_____

_____

_____

_____

Daily Planner

Date: _____

To do

Morning _____

_____

_____

_____

_____

_____

_____

Afternoon _____

_____

_____

_____

_____

_____

_____

Evening _____

_____

_____

_____

_____

_____

_____

_____

Goals

_____

_____

_____

_____

Appointments

_____

_____

Call / Email

_____

_____

Meal Planner

_____

_____

Water Intake

○ ○ ○ ○
○ ○ ○ ○

Steps _____

Notes

If you think you can't, you're right. Carol Bartz

_____

_____

_____

_____

_____

_____

_____

Daily Planner

Date: _____

To do

Morning _____
_____
_____
_____
_____
_____
_____
_____

Afternoon _____
_____
_____
_____
_____
_____
_____

Evening _____
_____
_____
_____
_____
_____
_____
_____

Goals
_____
_____
_____
_____
_____

Appointments
_____
_____
_____

Call / Email
_____
_____

Meal Planner
_____
_____

Water Intake
○ ○ ○ ○
○ ○ ○ ○

Steps _____

Notes

To do great things is difficult, but to command great things is more difficult. Friedrich Nietzsche
_____
_____
_____
_____
_____
_____
_____
_____

Daily Planner

Date: _____

To do

Morning _____

_____

_____

_____

_____

_____

_____

Afternoon _____

_____

_____

_____

_____

_____

_____

Evening _____

_____

_____

_____

_____

_____

_____

Goals

_____

_____

_____

_____

Appointments

_____

_____

Call / Email

_____

_____

Meal Planner

_____

_____

Water Intake

◯ ◯ ◯ ◯
◯ ◯ ◯ ◯

Steps _____

Notes

As we are liberated from our own fear, our presence automatically liberates others.
Nelson Mandela

_____

_____

_____

_____

_____

_____

_____

Daily Planner

Date: _____

To do

Morning _____
_____
_____
_____
_____
_____
_____

Afternoon _____
_____
_____
_____
_____
_____
_____

Evening _____
_____
_____
_____
_____
_____
_____
_____

Goals
_____
_____
_____
_____
_____

Appointments
_____
_____
_____

Call / Email
_____
_____

Meal Planner
_____
_____

Water Intake
◯ ◯ ◯ ◯
◯ ◯ ◯ ◯

Steps _____

Notes

An education isn't how much you have committed to memory, or even how much you know. It's being able to differentiate between what you know and what you don't. Anatole France
_____
_____
_____
_____
_____
_____

Daily Planner

Date: _____

To do

Morning _____
_____
_____
_____
_____

_____
_____
_____

Afternoon _____
_____
_____
_____
_____
_____
_____

Evening _____
_____
_____
_____
_____
_____
_____

Goals

_____
_____
_____
_____
_____
_____

Appointments

_____
_____
_____

Call / Email

_____
_____
_____

Meal Planner

_____
_____
_____

Water Intake

○ ○ ○ ○
○ ○ ○ ○

Steps _____

Notes

Our deepest fear is that we are powerful beyond measure. Marianne Williamson

_____
_____
_____
_____
_____
_____
_____

workout log

Week

Date : _____   Time : _____   Week : _____

Workout Day :   ①   ②   ③   ④   ⑤   ⑥   ⑦

Exercise	Reps	Set -1	Set -2	Set -3	Set -4	Set -5

Date : _____   Time : _____   Week : _____

Workout Day :   ①   ②   ③   ④   ⑤   ⑥   ⑦

Exercise	Reps	Set -1	Set -2	Set -3	Set -4	Set -5

Weight

Body Fat

Chest

Right Arm

Left Arm

Waist

Hips

Right Leg

Left Leg

To Do List This Week

Day _____

Date & Month _____

No.	To Do	Yes/No
_____	_____	☐ ☐
_____	_____	☐ ☐
_____	_____	☐ ☐
_____	_____	☐ ☐
_____	_____	☐ ☐
_____	_____	☐ ☐
_____	_____	☐ ☐
_____	_____	☐ ☐
_____	_____	☐ ☐
_____	_____	☐ ☐
_____	_____	☐ ☐
_____	_____	☐ ☐
_____	_____	☐ ☐
_____	_____	☐ ☐
_____	_____	☐ ☐
_____	_____	☐ ☐
_____	_____	☐ ☐
_____	_____	☐ ☐
_____	_____	☐ ☐
_____	_____	☐ ☐

Notes _____
_____

You can't blow an uncertain trumpet. Theodore Hesburgh

Daily Planner

Date: _____

To do

Morning _____

_____

_____

_____

_____

_____

_____

Afternoon _____

_____

_____

_____

_____

_____

_____

Evening _____

_____

_____

_____

_____

_____

_____

Goals

_____

_____

_____

_____

_____

Appointments

_____

_____

Call / Email

_____

_____

Meal Planner

_____

_____

_____

Water Intake

○ ○ ○ ○
○ ○ ○ ○

Steps _____

Notes

Leadership does not always wear the harness of compromise. Woodrow Wilson

_____

_____

_____

_____

_____

Daily Planner

Date: _____

To do

Morning _____

_____
_____
_____
_____
_____
_____
_____

Afternoon _____

_____
_____
_____
_____
_____
_____

Evening _____

_____
_____
_____
_____
_____
_____

Goals

_____
_____
_____
_____
_____

Appointments

_____
_____

Call / Email

_____
_____

Meal Planner

_____
_____

Water Intake

◯ ◯ ◯ ◯
◯ ◯ ◯ ◯

Steps _____

Notes

Be the change you want to see in the world.
Mahatma Gandhi

_____
_____
_____
_____
_____
_____

Daily Planner

Date: _____

To do

Morning _____

_____

_____

_____

_____

_____

_____

_____

Afternoon _____

_____

_____

_____

_____

_____

_____

_____

Evening _____

_____

_____

_____

_____

_____

_____

_____

Goals

_____

_____

_____

_____

_____

Appointments

_____

_____

Call / Email

_____

_____

Meal Planner

_____

_____

_____

Water Intake

◯ ◯ ◯

◯ ◯ ◯

Steps _____

Notes

"Change will not come if we wait for some other person or if we wait for some time. We are the ones we've been waiting for." Former President of the United States, Barack Obama

_____

_____

_____

_____

_____

_____

Daily Planner

Date: _____

To do

Morning _____

_____

_____

_____

_____

_____

_____

Afternoon _____

_____

_____

_____

_____

_____

_____

Evening _____

_____

_____

_____

_____

_____

_____

_____

Goals

_____

_____

_____

_____

Appointments

_____

_____

Call / Email

_____

_____

Meal Planner

_____

_____

Water Intake

◯ ◯ ◯ ◯
◯ ◯ ◯ ◯

Steps _____

Notes

"Don't count the days, make the days count."
Muhammad Ali

_____

_____

_____

_____

_____

_____

_____

Date: _____

To do

Morning _____

_____

_____

_____

_____

_____

_____

Afternoon _____

_____

_____

_____

_____

_____

_____

Evening _____

_____

_____

_____

_____

_____

Goals

_____

_____

_____

_____

_____

Appointments

_____

_____

Call / Email

_____

_____

Meal Planner

_____

_____

Water Intake

○ ○ ○
○ ○ ○

Steps _____

Notes

"Stumbling is not falling." Malcolm X

_____

_____

_____

_____

_____

_____

_____

Daily Planner

Date: _____

To do

Morning _____
_____
_____
_____
_____
_____
_____
_____

Afternoon _____
_____
_____
_____
_____
_____
_____
_____

Evening _____
_____
_____
_____
_____
_____
_____
_____

Goals
_____
_____
_____
_____

Appointments
_____
_____

Call / Email
_____
_____

Meal Planner
_____
_____

Water Intake
○ ○ ○
○ ○ ○

Steps _____

Notes
"My mission in life is not merely to survive, but to thrive; and to do so with some passion, some compassion, some humor and some style."
Maya Angelou
_____
_____
_____
_____
_____

Daily Planner

Date: _____

To do

Morning _____
_____
_____
_____
_____
_____
_____
_____

Afternoon _____
_____
_____
_____
_____
_____
_____

Evening _____
_____
_____
_____
_____
_____
_____

Goals

_____
_____
_____
_____
_____

Appointments

_____
_____
_____

Call / Email

_____
_____
_____

Meal Planner

_____
_____

Water Intake

○ ○ ○
○ ○ ○

Steps _____

Notes

"You don't make progress by standing on the sidelines, whimpering and complaining. You make progress by implementing ideas." Shirley Chisholm

_____
_____
_____
_____
_____
_____
_____

workout log

Week

Date: [   ]   Time: [   ]   Week: [   ]

Workout Day:	①	②	③	④	⑤	⑥	⑦

Exercise	Reps	Set -1	Set -2	Set -3	Set -4	Set -5

Date: [   ]   Time: [   ]   Week: [   ]

Workout Day:	①	②	③	④	⑤	⑥	⑦

Exercise	Reps	Set -1	Set -2	Set -3	Set -4	Set -5

Weight

Body Fat

Chest

Right Arm

Left Arm

Waist

Hips

Right Leg

Left Leg

To Do List This Week

Day _____

Date & Month _____

No.	To Do	Yes/No
____	_____	☐ ☐
____	_____	☐ ☐
____	_____	☐ ☐
____	_____	☐ ☐
____	_____	☐ ☐
____	_____	☐ ☐
____	_____	☐ ☐
____	_____	☐ ☐
____	_____	☐ ☐
____	_____	☐ ☐
____	_____	☐ ☐
____	_____	☐ ☐
____	_____	☐ ☐
____	_____	☐ ☐
____	_____	☐ ☐
____	_____	☐ ☐
____	_____	☐ ☐
____	_____	☐ ☐
____	_____	☐ ☐
____	_____	☐ ☐

Notes _____

_____

_____

_____

Daily Planner

Date: _____

To do

Morning _____

_____
_____
_____
_____
_____
_____
_____

Afternoon _____

_____
_____
_____
_____
_____
_____

Evening _____

_____
_____
_____
_____
_____
_____
_____

Goals

_____
_____
_____
_____
_____

Appointments

_____
_____
_____

Call / Email

_____
_____
_____

Meal Planner

_____
_____

Water Intake

◯ ◯ ◯
◯ ◯ ◯

Steps _____

Notes

Be the peace you wish to see in the world. Martin Luther King, Jr.

_____
_____
_____
_____
_____
_____

Daily Planner

Date: _____

To do

Morning _____

_____

_____

_____

_____

_____

_____

_____

Afternoon _____

_____

_____

_____

_____

_____

_____

Evening _____

_____

_____

_____

_____

_____

_____

Goals

_____

_____

_____

_____

_____

Appointments

_____

_____

_____

Call / Email

_____

_____

_____

Meal Planner

_____

_____

_____

Water Intake

○ ○ ○ ○
○ ○ ○ ○

Steps _____

Notes

There is nothing enlightened about shrinking so that other people will not feel secure around you. We are all meant to shine, as children do. We were born to make manifest the glory of God that is within us. It is not just in some of us; it is in everyone and as we let our own light shine, we unconsciously give others permission to do the same. As we are liberated from our own fear, our presence automatically liberates others. Marianne Williamson

_____

_____

_____

_____

Daily Planner

Date: _____

To do

Morning _____

_____

_____

_____

_____

_____

_____

_____

Afternoon _____

_____

_____

_____

_____

_____

_____

Evening _____

_____

_____

_____

_____

_____

Goals

_____

_____

_____

_____

_____

Appointments

_____

_____

_____

Call / Email

_____

_____

_____

Meal Planner

_____

_____

_____

Water Intake

○ ○ ○ ○

○ ○ ○ ○

Steps _____

Notes

What chance gathers, she easily scatters. A great person attracts great people and knows how to hold them together. Johann Wolfgang von Goethe

_____

_____

_____

_____

_____

_____

_____

Daily Planner

Date: _____

To do

Morning _____

_____

_____

_____

_____

_____

_____

_____

Afternoon _____

_____

_____

_____

_____

_____

_____

Evening _____

_____

_____

_____

_____

_____

_____

Goals

_____

_____

_____

_____

_____

Appointments

_____

_____

Call / Email

_____

_____

Meal Planner

_____

_____

Water Intake

○ ○ ○ ○
○ ○ ○ ○

Steps _____

Notes

Do not follow where the path may lead.
Ralph Waldo Emerson

_____

_____

_____

_____

_____

_____

_____

_____

Daily Planner

Date: _____

To do

Morning _____

_____
_____
_____
_____
_____
_____
_____

Afternoon _____

_____
_____
_____
_____
_____

Evening _____

_____
_____
_____
_____
_____
_____
_____

Goals

_____
_____
_____
_____
_____

Appointments

_____
_____
_____

Call / Email

_____
_____
_____

Meal Planner

_____
_____

Water Intake

○ ○ ○
○ ○ ○

Steps _____

Notes

A leader is best when people barely know that he exists. Witter Bynner

_____
_____
_____
_____
_____
_____
_____

Daily Planner

Date: _____

To do

Morning _____

_____

_____

_____

_____

_____

_____

_____

Afternoon _____

_____

_____

_____

_____

_____

_____

_____

Evening _____

_____

_____

_____

_____

_____

_____

Goals

_____

_____

_____

_____

_____

Appointments

_____

_____

Call / Email

_____

_____

Meal Planner

_____

_____

_____

Water Intake

○ ○ ○ ○
○ ○ ○ ○

Steps _____

Notes

Twenty years from now you will be more disappointed by the things that you didn't do then by the ones you did do. So throw off the bowlines. Sail away from the safe harbor. Catch the trade winds in your sails. Explore. Dream. Discover. H. Jackson Brown, Jr.

_____

_____

_____

_____

_____

Daily Planner

Date: _____

To do

Morning _____

_____
_____
_____
_____
_____
_____
_____

Afternoon _____

_____
_____
_____
_____
_____
_____

Evening _____

_____
_____
_____
_____
_____
_____
_____

Goals

_____
_____
_____
_____
_____

Appointments

_____
_____
_____

Call / Email

_____
_____
_____

Meal Planner

_____
_____
_____

Water Intake

◯ ◯ ◯ ◯
◯ ◯ ◯ ◯

Steps _____

Notes

A good general not only sees the way to
victory; he knows when victory is impossible.
Polybius

_____
_____
_____
_____
_____
_____
_____

workout log

Week

Date: _____ Time: _____ Week: _____

Workout Day: ① ② ③ ④ ⑤ ⑥ ⑦

Exercise	Reps	Set -1	Set -2	Set -3	Set -4	Set -5

Date: _____ Time: _____ Week: _____

Workout Day: ① ② ③ ④ ⑤ ⑥ ⑦

Exercise	Reps	Set -1	Set -2	Set -3	Set -4	Set -5

Weight

Body Fat

Chest

Right Arm

Left Arm

Waist

Hips

Right Leg

Left Leg

MY MEETING NOTES

MEETING NAME & DATE -

ATTENDEES -

NEXT STEPS / DEADLINES -

MEETING NOTES -

"Character, not circumstances, makes the man." Booker T. Washington

MY MEETING NOTES

MEETING NAME & DATE -

ATTENDEES -

NEXT STEPS / DEADLINES -

MEETING NOTES -

_____
_____
_____
_____
_____
_____
_____
_____
_____
_____
_____
_____
_____
_____
_____
_____
_____
_____
_____
_____
_____

"If there's a book you want to read, but it hasn't been written yet, then you must write it."
Toni Morrison

MY MEETING NOTES

MEETING NAME & DATE -

ATTENDEES -

NEXT STEPS / DEADLINES -

MEETING NOTES -

"When you do the common things in life in an uncommon way, you will command the attention of the world." George Washington Carver

MY MEETING NOTES

MEETING NAME & DATE -

ATTENDEES -

NEXT STEPS / DEADLINES -

MEETING NOTES -

"You can't just sit there and wait for people to give you that golden dream. You've got to get out there and make it happen for yourself." Diana Ross

MY MEETING NOTES

MEETING NAME & DATE -

ATTENDEES -

NEXT STEPS / DEADLINES -

MEETING NOTES -

"I think people who have faults are a lot more interesting than people who are perfect."
Spike Lee

MY MEETING NOTES

MEETING NAME & DATE -

ATTENDEES -

NEXT STEPS / DEADLINES -

MEETING NOTES -

_____

_____

_____

_____

_____

_____

_____

_____

_____

_____

_____

_____

_____

_____

_____

_____

_____

_____

_____

"Each of you, as an individual, must pick your own goals. Listen to others, but do not become a blind follower." Thurgood Marshall

MY MEETING NOTES

MEETING NAME & DATE -

ATTENDEES -

NEXT STEPS / DEADLINES -

MEETING NOTES -

"How you climb a mountain is more important than reaching the top."

MY MEETING NOTES

MEETING NAME & DATE -

ATTENDEES -

NEXT STEPS / DEADLINES -

MEETING NOTES -

"We are enough to ensure we have all of the opportunities of the American dream, and we will show it to each other through our actions and through our words and through our deeds."
Robert F. Smith

MY MEETING NOTES

MEETING NAME & DATE -

ATTENDEES -

NEXT STEPS / DEADLINES -

MEETING NOTES -

"When you accept that failure is a good thing, it can actually be a huge propeller toward success." - Whitney Wolfe Herd

MONTHLY REVIEW

THIS MONTH I ACHIEVED

_____
_____
_____
_____
_____
_____
_____

WHAT WORKED

_____
_____
_____

WHAT DIDN'T WORK

_____
_____
_____

DO MORE OF

DO LESS OF

MONTHLY REVIEW

THIS MONTH I ACHIEVED

WHAT WORKED

WHAT DIDN'T WORK

DO MORE OF	DO LESS OF

NOVEMBER

YOUR FITNESS SAMPLE

MON
LEGS

Stretching and warm-up
25 Squats
25 Sumo Squats
Repeat above March in place for 20 sec
Stretch muscles
Relax

TUES
ABS

Stretching and warm-up
20 Standing Oblique Twists
30-second Floor Plank
Repeat above
March in place for 20 seconds
Stretch muscles
Relax

WED
ARMS

Stretching and warm-up
25 Push-ups
20 Wall Tricep Pushes
Repeat above
March in place for 20 seconds
Stretch muscles
Relax

THURS
CARDIO

Stretching and warm-up
50 Jumping Jacks
30-second Sprint in place
Repeat above
March in place for 20 seconds
Stretch muscles
Relax

FRI
COMBO

Stretching and warm-up
10 Squats & 10 Sumo Squats
10 Standing Oblique Twists
March in place for 20 seconds
20 Push-ups
25 Jumping Jacks
March in place for 20 seconds
Stretch muscles
Relax

SAT
YOUR PICK

Choose from Day 1-4
to work on your chosen area:
Legs
Abs
Arms or
Cardio

SUN
REST

Take a break!
You deserve it.

workout log

Week

Date : _____ Time : _____ Week : _____

Workout Day : ① ② ③ ④ ⑤ ⑥ ⑦

Exercise	Reps	Set -1	Set -2	Set -3	Set -4	Set -5

Date : _____ Time : _____ Week : _____

Workout Day : ① ② ③ ④ ⑤ ⑥ ⑦

Exercise	Reps	Set -1	Set -2	Set -3	Set -4	Set -5

Weight

Body Fat

Chest

Right Arm

Left Arm

Waist

Hips

Right Leg

Left Leg

THIS MONTH'S LIST

Month: November Year: _____

Potential Items to Plan/Schedule

District Board Mtg
District Principal Mtg
Plan & Schedule Vertical Team Mtg
Parent Conferences
LPACS/ELLs/ARDs
Progress Reports/Report Cards
Master Schedule Review
Team Leader/Dept Chair Mtg
Campus Admin Mtg
Professional Learning Community (PLC)
Athletic Event Admin Coverage Schedule
Teachers I need to meet with (observe/walkthrough)

Potential Assessments

ASVAB
Universal GT/CogAT/Iowa
High Frequency Word Exam (Grade 1-2)
State Assessment Practice

Additions

Shared Decision Making Council (SDMC)
Thanksgiving Break
State Testing Planning for High School in December

_____
_____
_____
_____
_____
_____
_____
_____
_____
_____

MONTHLY PLANNER
MONTH: _____

MONDAY	TUESDAY	WEDNESDAY	THURSDAY	FRIDAY	SATURDAY	SUNDAY

PRIORITY

To Do List This Week

Day _____

Date & Month _____

No.	To Do	Yes/No
		☐ ☐
		☐ ☐
		☐ ☐
		☐ ☐
		☐ ☐
		☐ ☐
		☐ ☐
		☐ ☐
		☐ ☐
		☐ ☐
		☐ ☐
		☐ ☐
		☐ ☐
		☐ ☐
		☐ ☐
		☐ ☐
		☐ ☐
		☐ ☐
		☐ ☐
		☐ ☐

Notes _____

_____

_____

_____

Daily Planner

Date: _____

To do

Morning _____
_____
_____
_____
_____
_____
_____
_____

Afternoon _____
_____
_____
_____
_____
_____

Evening _____
_____
_____
_____
_____
_____
_____

Goals
_____
_____
_____
_____
_____

Appointments
_____
_____

Call / Email
_____
_____

Meal Planner
_____
_____

Water Intake
○ ○ ○ ○
○ ○ ○ ○

Steps _____

Notes
You manage things, you lead people. We went overboard on management and forgot about leadership. It might help if we ran the MBSs out of Washington. Grace Hopper
_____
_____
_____
_____
_____
_____
_____

Daily Planner

Date: _____

To do

Morning _____

_____

_____

_____

_____

_____

_____

_____

Afternoon _____

_____

_____

_____

_____

_____

_____

Evening _____

_____

_____

_____

_____

_____

_____

Goals

_____

_____

_____

_____

Appointments

_____

_____

Call / Email

_____

_____

Meal Planner

_____

_____

Water Intake

◯ ◯ ◯
◯ ◯ ◯

Steps _____

Notes

We were born to make manifest the glory of God within us. Marianne Williamson

_____

_____

_____

_____

_____

_____

Daily Planner

Date: _____

To do

Morning _____

_____

_____

_____

_____

_____

_____

_____

Afternoon _____

_____

_____

_____

_____

_____

_____

Evening _____

_____

_____

_____

_____

_____

_____

Goals

_____

_____

_____

_____

Appointments

_____

_____

Call / Email

_____

_____

Meal Planner

_____

_____

Water Intake

○ ○ ○
○ ○ ○

Steps _____

Notes

Your playing small does not serve the world. Who are you not to be great? Marianne Williamson

_____

_____

_____

_____

_____

_____

_____

Daily Planner

Date: _____

To do

Morning _____

_____

_____

_____

_____

_____

_____

_____

Afternoon _____

_____

_____

_____

_____

_____

_____

Evening _____

_____

_____

_____

_____

_____

_____

_____

Goals

_____

_____

_____

_____

_____

Appointments

_____

_____

Call / Email

_____

_____

Meal Planner

_____

_____

Water Intake

○ ○ ○ ○
○ ○ ○ ○

Steps _____

Notes

Carefully watch your thoughts, for they become your words. Manage and watch your words, for they become your actions. Consider and judge your actions, for they become your habits. Acknowledge and watch your habits, for they shall become your values. Understand and embrace your values, for they become your destiny.
Mahatma Gandhi

_____

_____

_____

_____

Daily Planner

Date: _____

To do

Morning _____
_____
_____
_____
_____
_____
_____
_____

Afternoon _____
_____
_____
_____
_____
_____
_____

Evening _____
_____
_____
_____
_____
_____
_____

Goals

_____
_____
_____
_____
_____

Appointments

_____
_____
_____

Call / Email

_____
_____
_____

Meal Planner

_____
_____
_____

Water Intake

◯ ◯ ◯ ◯
◯ ◯ ◯ ◯

Steps _____

Notes

Relationships are based on four principles:
Respect, Understanding, Acceptance, and
Appreciation. Mahatma Gandhi

_____
_____
_____
_____
_____
_____
_____
_____

Daily Planner

Date: _____

To do

Morning _____

_____

_____

_____

_____

_____

_____

_____

Afternoon _____

_____

_____

_____

_____

_____

_____

Evening _____

_____

_____

_____

_____

_____

_____

Goals

_____

_____

_____

_____

_____

Appointments

_____

_____

Call / Email

_____

_____

Meal Planner

_____

_____

Water Intake

○ ○ ○ ○
○ ○ ○ ○

Steps _____

Notes

There are two days in the year that we can not do anything, yesterday and tomorrow.
Mahatma Gandhi

_____

_____

_____

_____

_____

_____

_____

Daily Planner

Date: _____

To do

Morning _____

_____
_____
_____
_____
_____
_____
_____
_____

Afternoon _____

_____
_____
_____
_____
_____
_____

Evening _____

_____
_____
_____
_____
_____
_____
_____
_____

Goals

_____
_____
_____
_____
_____

Appointments

_____
_____

Call / Email

_____
_____

Meal Planner

_____
_____

Water Intake

◯ ◯ ◯ ◯
◯ ◯ ◯ ◯

Steps _____

Notes

The true measure of any society can be found in how it treats its most vulnerable members.
Mahatma Gandhi

_____
_____
_____
_____
_____
_____
_____

workout log

Week

Date: _____ Time: _____ Week: _____

Workout Day: ① ② ③ ④ ⑤ ⑥ ⑦

Exercise	Reps	Set -1	Set -2	Set -3	Set -4	Set -5

Date: _____ Time: _____ Week: _____

Workout Day: ① ② ③ ④ ⑤ ⑥ ⑦

Exercise	Reps	Set -1	Set -2	Set -3	Set -4	Set -5

Weight

Body Fat

Chest

Right Arm

Left Arm

Waist

Hips

Right Leg

Left Leg

To Do List This Week

Day _____

Date & Month _____

No.	To Do	Yes/No	
___	_____	☐	☐
___	_____	☐	☐
___	_____	☐	☐
___	_____	☐	☐
___	_____	☐	☐
___	_____	☐	☐
___	_____	☐	☐
___	_____	☐	☐
___	_____	☐	☐
___	_____	☐	☐
___	_____	☐	☐
___	_____	☐	☐
___	_____	☐	☐
___	_____	☐	☐
___	_____	☐	☐
___	_____	☐	☐
___	_____	☐	☐
___	_____	☐	☐
___	_____	☐	☐

Notes _____

_____

_____

_____

Daily Planner

Date: _____

To do

Morning _____

_____

_____

_____

_____

_____

_____

_____

Afternoon _____

_____

_____

_____

_____

_____

_____

Evening _____

_____

_____

_____

_____

_____

_____

Goals

_____

_____

_____

_____

_____

Appointments

_____

_____

Call / Email

_____

_____

Meal Planner

_____

_____

Water Intake

○ ○ ○

○ ○ ○

Steps _____

Notes

Our greatest ability as humans is not to change the world, but to change ourselves. Mahatma Gandhi

_____

_____

_____

_____

_____

_____

_____

Daily Planner

Date: _____

To do

Morning _____

_____

_____

_____

_____

_____

_____

Afternoon _____

_____

_____

_____

_____

_____

_____

_____

Evening _____

_____

_____

_____

_____

_____

_____

Goals

_____

_____

_____

_____

_____

Appointments

_____

_____

Call / Email

_____

_____

Meal Planner

_____

_____

Water Intake

◯ ◯ ◯ ◯
◯ ◯ ◯ ◯

Steps _____

Notes

Confucius, teacher and philosopher: "Real knowledge is to know the extent of one's ignorance."

_____

_____

_____

_____

_____

_____

_____

Daily Planner

Date: _____

To do

Morning _____

_____

_____

_____

_____

_____

_____

_____

Afternoon _____

_____

_____

_____

_____

_____

_____

Evening _____

_____

_____

_____

_____

_____

_____

Goals

_____

_____

_____

_____

_____

_____

Appointments

_____

_____

_____

Call / Email

_____

_____

Meal Planner

_____

_____

Water Intake

○ ○ ○ ○
○ ○ ○ ○

Steps _____

Notes

It's easy to stand in a crowd, but it takes courage to stand alone. Mahatma Gandhi

_____

_____

_____

_____

_____

_____

_____

_____

Daily Planner

Date: _____

To do

Morning _____
_____
_____
_____
_____
_____
_____
_____
_____

Afternoon _____
_____
_____
_____
_____
_____
_____
_____

Evening _____
_____
_____
_____
_____
_____
_____
_____

Goals

_____
_____
_____
_____

Appointments

_____
_____

Call / Email

_____
_____

Meal Planner

_____
_____

Water Intake

○ ○ ○
○ ○ ○

Steps _____

Notes

Henry Louis Gates, Jr., historian, and filmmaker:
"The first step toward tolerance is respect and the
first step toward respect is knowledge."

_____
_____
_____
_____
_____
_____

Daily Planner

Date: _____

To do

Morning _____
_____
_____
_____
_____
_____
_____
_____

Afternoon _____
_____
_____
_____
_____
_____
_____

Evening _____
_____
_____
_____
_____
_____
_____

Goals

_____
_____
_____
_____

Appointments

_____
_____

Call / Email

_____
_____

Meal Planner

_____
_____

Water Intake

○ ○ ○ ○
○ ○ ○ ○

Steps _____

Notes

Barack Obama, 44th President of the United States: "In a global economy where the most valuable skill you can sell is your knowledge, a good education is no longer just a pathway to opportunity - it is a prerequisite."

_____
_____
_____
_____
_____
_____

Daily Planner

Date: _____

To do

Morning _____

_____

_____

_____

_____

_____

_____

Afternoon _____

_____

_____

_____

_____

_____

_____

Evening _____

_____

_____

_____

_____

_____

_____

Goals

_____

_____

_____

_____

_____

Appointments

_____

_____

_____

Call / Email

_____

_____

_____

Meal Planner

_____

_____

Water Intake

○ ○ ○ ○
○ ○ ○ ○

Steps _____

Notes

Arne Duncan, former U.S. Secretary of Education:
"Even in a time of fiscal austerity, education is more
than just an expense."

_____

_____

_____

_____

_____

_____

_____

Daily Planner

Date: _____

To do

Morning _____
_____
_____
_____
_____
_____
_____
_____

Afternoon _____
_____
_____
_____
_____
_____
_____

Evening _____
_____
_____
_____
_____
_____
_____
_____

Goals

_____
_____
_____
_____
_____

Appointments

_____
_____

Call / Email

_____
_____

Meal Planner

_____
_____

Water Intake

○ ○ ○ ○
○ ○ ○ ○

Steps _____

Notes

W. E. B. Du Bois, American civil rights activist and sociologist: "Education is that whole system of human training within and without the school house walls, which molds and develops men."

_____
_____
_____
_____
_____
_____

workout log

Week

Date: _____ Time: _____ Week: _____

Workout Day: ① ② ③ ④ ⑤ ⑥ ⑦

Exercise	Reps	Set-1	Set-2	Set-3	Set-4	Set-5

Date: _____ Time: _____ Week: _____

Workout Day: ① ② ③ ④ ⑤ ⑥ ⑦

Exercise	Reps	Set-1	Set-2	Set-3	Set-4	Set-5

Weight

Body Fat

Chest

Right Arm

Left Arm

Waist

Hips

Right Leg

Left Leg

To Do List This Week

Day _____

Date & Month _____

No.	To Do	Yes/No	
_____	_____	☐	☐
_____	_____	☐	☐
_____	_____	☐	☐
_____	_____	☐	☐
_____	_____	☐	☐
_____	_____	☐	☐
_____	_____	☐	☐
_____	_____	☐	☐
_____	_____	☐	☐
_____	_____	☐	☐
_____	_____	☐	☐
_____	_____	☐	☐
_____	_____	☐	☐
_____	_____	☐	☐
_____	_____	☐	☐
_____	_____	☐	☐
_____	_____	☐	☐
_____	_____	☐	☐
_____	_____	☐	☐
_____	_____	☐	☐

Notes _____
_____
_____
_____

Daily Planner

Date: _____

To do

Morning _____

_____

_____

_____

_____

_____

_____

_____

Afternoon _____

_____

_____

_____

_____

_____

_____

Evening _____

_____

_____

_____

_____

_____

_____

Goals

_____

_____

_____

_____

_____

_____

Appointments

_____

_____

_____

Call / Email

_____

_____

_____

Meal Planner

_____

_____

_____

Water Intake

◯ ◯ ◯ ◯
◯ ◯ ◯ ◯

Steps _____

Notes

Anne Sullivan, instructor and lifelong companion of Helen Keller: "Children require guidance and sympathy far more than instruction."

_____

_____

_____

_____

_____

_____

_____

Daily Planner

Date: _____

To do

Morning _____
_____
_____
_____
_____
_____
_____
_____

Afternoon _____
_____
_____
_____
_____
_____
_____

Evening _____
_____
_____
_____
_____
_____
_____

Goals
_____
_____
_____
_____

Appointments
_____
_____

Call / Email
_____
_____

Meal Planner
_____
_____

Water Intake
○ ○ ○
○ ○ ○

Steps _____

Notes

Helen Keller, author, political activist, and lecturer: "The highest result of education is tolerance."

_____
_____
_____
_____
_____
_____

Date: _____

To do

Morning _____

_____

_____

_____

_____

_____

_____

_____

Afternoon _____

_____

_____

_____

_____

_____

_____

_____

Evening _____

_____

_____

_____

_____

_____

_____

Goals

_____

_____

_____

_____

Appointments

_____

_____

Call / Email

_____

_____

Meal Planner

_____

_____

Water Intake

○ ○ ○ ○
○ ○ ○ ○

Steps _____

Notes

George Washington Carver, botanist and inventor: "Education is the key to unlock the golden door of freedom."

_____

_____

_____

_____

_____

_____

Daily Planner

Date: _____

To do

Morning _____
_____
_____
_____
_____
_____
_____
_____

Afternoon _____
_____
_____
_____
_____
_____
_____
_____

Evening _____
_____
_____
_____
_____
_____
_____
_____

Goals
_____
_____
_____
_____
_____

Appointments
_____
_____

Call / Email
_____
_____

Meal Planner
_____
_____

Water Intake
◯ ◯ ◯ ◯
◯ ◯ ◯ ◯

Steps _____

Notes
Aristotle, ancient Greek philosopher and scientist: "Educating the mind without educating the heart is no education at all."
_____
_____
_____
_____
_____
_____
_____

Daily Planner

Date: _____

To do

Morning _____

_____

_____

_____

_____

_____

_____

_____

Afternoon _____

_____

_____

_____

_____

_____

_____

Evening _____

_____

_____

_____

_____

_____

_____

Goals

_____

_____

_____

_____

_____

Appointments

_____

_____

_____

Call / Email

_____

_____

_____

Meal Planner

_____

_____

Water Intake

◯ ◯ ◯ ◯
◯ ◯ ◯ ◯

Steps _____

Notes

Find purpose. The means will follow.
Mahatma Gandhi

_____

_____

_____

_____

_____

_____

_____

Daily Planner

Date: _____

To do

Morning _____

_____

_____

_____

_____

_____

_____

_____

Afternoon _____

_____

_____

_____

_____

_____

_____

Evening _____

_____

_____

_____

_____

_____

_____

Goals

_____

_____

_____

_____

Appointments

_____

_____

Call / Email

_____

_____

Meal Planner

_____

_____

Water Intake

○ ○ ○ ○
○ ○ ○ ○

Steps _____

Notes

It's not too late at all. You just don't yet know what you are capable of. Mahatma Gandhi

_____

_____

_____

_____

_____

_____

_____

Daily Planner

Date: _____

To do

Morning _____
_____
_____
_____
_____
_____
_____
_____

Afternoon _____
_____
_____
_____
_____
_____
_____

Evening _____
_____
_____
_____
_____
_____
_____

Goals
_____
_____
_____
_____
_____

Appointments
_____
_____
_____

Call / Email
_____
_____

Meal Planner
_____
_____

Water Intake
○ ○ ○
○ ○ ○

Steps _____

Notes
The best way to find yourself is to lose yourself in the service of others. Mahatma Gandhi
_____
_____
_____
_____
_____
_____

workout log

Week

Date: [   ] Time: [   ] Week: [   ]

Workout Day: ① ② ③ ④ ⑤ ⑥ ⑦

Exercise	Reps	Set -1	Set -2	Set -3	Set -4	Set -5

Date: [   ] Time: [   ] Week: [   ]

Workout Day: ① ② ③ ④ ⑤ ⑥ ⑦

Exercise	Reps	Set -1	Set -2	Set -3	Set -4	Set -5

Weight

Body Fat

Chest

Right Arm

Left Arm

Waist

Hips

Right Leg

Left Leg

To Do List This Week

Day _____

Date & Month _____

No.	To Do	Yes/No	
_____	_____	☐	☐
_____	_____	☐	☐
_____	_____	☐	☐
_____	_____	☐	☐
_____	_____	☐	☐
_____	_____	☐	☐
_____	_____	☐	☐
_____	_____	☐	☐
_____	_____	☐	☐
_____	_____	☐	☐
_____	_____	☐	☐
_____	_____	☐	☐
_____	_____	☐	☐
_____	_____	☐	☐
_____	_____	☐	☐
_____	_____	☐	☐
_____	_____	☐	☐
_____	_____	☐	☐
_____	_____	☐	☐
_____	_____	☐	☐

Notes _____

_____

_____

_____

Daily Planner

Date: _____

To do

Morning _____
_____
_____
_____
_____
_____
_____

Afternoon _____
_____
_____
_____
_____
_____
_____

Evening _____
_____
_____
_____
_____
_____
_____
_____

Goals
_____
_____
_____
_____

Appointments
_____
_____

Call / Email
_____
_____

Meal Planner
_____
_____

Water Intake
○ ○ ○
○ ○ ○

Steps _____

Notes
"I don't create companies for the sake of creating companies, but to get things done."
_____
_____
_____
_____
_____
_____
_____

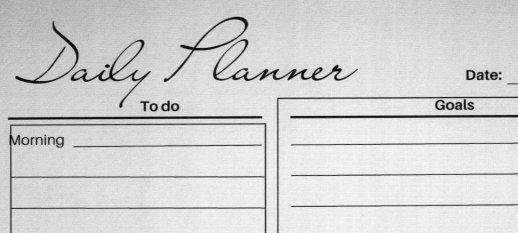

Daily Planner

Date: _____

To do

Morning _____

Afternoon _____

Evening _____

Goals

Appointments

Call / Email

Meal Planner

Water Intake

○ ○ ○ ○
○ ○ ○ ○

Steps _____

Notes

"You're never too young or too old to be a mentor."

Daily Planner

Date: _____

To do

Morning _____
_____
_____
_____
_____
_____

Afternoon _____
_____
_____
_____
_____
_____

Evening _____
_____
_____
_____
_____

Goals
_____
_____
_____
_____

Appointments
_____
_____

Call / Email
_____
_____

Meal Planner
_____
_____

Water Intake
◯ ◯ ◯ ◯
◯ ◯ ◯ ◯

Steps _____

Notes

"Be thankful for what you have; you'll end up having more. If you concentrate on what you don't have, you will never, ever have enough." -- Oprah Winfrey
_____
_____
_____
_____
_____
_____

Daily Planner

Date: _____

To do

Morning _____

_____

_____

_____

_____

_____

_____

Afternoon _____

_____

_____

_____

_____

_____

Evening _____

_____

_____

_____

_____

_____

Goals

_____

_____

_____

_____

Appointments

_____

_____

Call / Email

_____

_____

Meal Planner

_____

_____

Water Intake

○ ○ ○ ○
○ ○ ○ ○

Steps _____

Notes

"If a fellow isn't thankful for what he's got, he isn't likely to be thankful for what he's going to get." -- Frank A. Clark

_____

_____

_____

_____

_____

_____

_____

Daily Planner

Date: _____

To do

Morning _____
_____
_____
_____

_____

_____

_____

_____

Afternoon _____
_____

_____

_____

_____

_____

_____

Evening _____
_____

_____

_____

_____

_____

Goals
_____
_____
_____
_____

Appointments
_____
_____

Call / Email
_____
_____

Meal Planner
_____
_____

Water Intake
○ ○ ○ ○
○ ○ ○ ○

Steps _____

Notes
"Let gratitude be the pillow upon which you kneel to say your nightly prayer. And let faith be the bridge you build to overcome evil and welcome good." -- Maya Angelou
_____
_____
_____
_____
_____
_____
_____

Daily Planner

Date: _____

To do

Morning _____

_____

_____

_____

_____

_____

_____

_____

Afternoon _____

_____

_____

_____

_____

_____

_____

Evening _____

_____

_____

_____

_____

_____

Goals

_____

_____

_____

_____

Appointments

_____

_____

Call / Email

_____

_____

Meal Planner

_____

_____

Water Intake

◯ ◯ ◯ ◯
◯ ◯ ◯ ◯

Steps _____

Notes

"Cultivate the habit of being grateful for every good thing that comes to you, and to give thanks continuously. And because all things have contributed to your advancement, you should include all things in your gratitude." -- Ralph Waldo Emerson

_____

_____

_____

_____

_____

Daily Planner

Date: _____

To do

Morning _____

_____

_____

_____

_____

_____

_____

_____

Afternoon _____

_____

_____

_____

_____

_____

_____

Evening _____

_____

_____

_____

_____

_____

_____

_____

Goals

_____

_____

_____

_____

Appointments

_____

_____

Call / Email

_____

_____

Meal Planner

_____

_____

Water Intake

◯ ◯ ◯
◯ ◯ ◯

Steps _____

Notes

"Gratitude is not only the greatest of virtues, but the parent of all others." -- Marcus Tullius Cicero

_____

_____

_____

_____

_____

_____

_____

_____

workout log

Week

Date : _____ Time : _____ Week : _____

Workout Day : ① ② ③ ④ ⑤ ⑥ ⑦

Exercise	Reps	Set-1	Set-2	Set-3	Set-4	Set-5

Date : _____ Time : _____ Week : _____

Workout Day : ① ② ③ ④ ⑤ ⑥ ⑦

Exercise	Reps	Set-1	Set-2	Set-3	Set-4	Set-5

Weight

Body Fat

Chest

Right Arm

Left Arm

Waist

Hips

Right Leg

Left Leg

MONTHLY REVIEW

THIS MONTH I ACHIEVED

_____

_____

_____

_____

_____

_____

_____

_____

_____

WHAT WORKED

_____

_____

_____

_____

WHAT DIDN'T WORK

_____

_____

_____

_____

DO MORE OF	DO LESS OF

MONTHLY REVIEW

THIS MONTH I ACHIEVED

_____

_____

_____

_____

_____

_____

_____

_____

WHAT WORKED

_____

_____

_____

_____

WHAT DIDN'T WORK

_____

_____

_____

_____

DO MORE OF	DO LESS OF

DECEMBER

THIS MONTH'S LIST
Month: December Year: _____

Potential Items to Plan/Schedule
District Board Mtg
District Principal Mtg
Plan & Schedule Vertical Team Mtg
Parent Conferences
LPACS/ELLs/ARDs
Progress Reports/Report Cards
Master Schedule Review
Team Leader/Dept Chair Mtg
Campus Admin Mtg
Professional Learning Community (PLC)
Athletic Event Admin Coverage Schedule

Potential Assessments
ASVAB
Universal GT/CogAT/Iowa
High Frequency Word Exam (Grade 1-2)
State Assessment Practice

Additions
Shared Decision Making Council (SDMC)
Winter Break

_____
_____
_____
_____
_____
_____
_____

MONTHLY PLANNER
MONTH: _____

MONDAY	TUESDAY	WEDNESDAY	THURSDAY	FRIDAY	SATURDAY	SUNDAY

PRIORITY

To Do List This Week

Day _____

Date & Month _____

No.	To Do	Yes/No
___	_____	☐ ☐
___	_____	☐ ☐
___	_____	☐ ☐
___	_____	☐ ☐
___	_____	☐ ☐
___	_____	☐ ☐
___	_____	☐ ☐
___	_____	☐ ☐
___	_____	☐ ☐
___	_____	☐ ☐
___	_____	☐ ☐
___	_____	☐ ☐
___	_____	☐ ☐
___	_____	☐ ☐
___	_____	☐ ☐
___	_____	☐ ☐
___	_____	☐ ☐
___	_____	☐ ☐
___	_____	☐ ☐
___	_____	☐ ☐
___	_____	☐ ☐

Notes _____

_____

_____

_____

Daily Planner

Date: _____

To do

Morning _____

_____

_____

_____

_____

_____

_____

_____

Afternoon _____

_____

_____

_____

_____

_____

_____

_____

Evening _____

_____

_____

_____

_____

_____

_____

_____

Goals

_____

_____

_____

_____

_____

Appointments

_____

_____

_____

Call / Email

_____

_____

Meal Planner

_____

_____

Water Intake

○ ○ ○ ○
○ ○ ○ ○

Steps _____

Notes

"The unthankful heart discovers no mercies; but the thankful heart will find, in every hour, some heavenly blessings." -- Henry Ward Beecher

_____

_____

_____

_____

_____

_____

_____

Date: _____

To do

Morning _____
_____
_____
_____
_____
_____
_____
_____

Afternoon _____
_____
_____
_____
_____
_____
_____

Evening _____
_____
_____
_____
_____
_____
_____

Goals

_____
_____
_____
_____
_____

Appointments

_____
_____
_____

Call / Email

_____
_____
_____

Meal Planner

_____
_____

Water Intake

◯ ◯ ◯ ◯
◯ ◯ ◯ ◯

Steps _____

Notes

"We must find time to stop and thank the people
who make a difference in our lives." -
John F. Kennedy

_____
_____
_____
_____
_____
_____
_____

Daily Planner

Date: _____

To do

Morning _____

_____

_____

_____

_____

_____

_____

_____

_____

Afternoon _____

_____

_____

_____

_____

_____

_____

_____

Evening _____

_____

_____

_____

_____

_____

_____

Goals

_____

_____

_____

_____

_____

Appointments

_____

_____

Call / Email

_____

_____

Meal Planner

_____

_____

Water Intake

◯ ◯ ◯
◯ ◯ ◯

Steps _____

Notes

"Thank you is the best prayer that anyone could say. I say that one a lot. Thank you expresses extreme gratitude, humility, understanding."
Alice Walker

_____

_____

_____

_____

_____

_____

_____

_____

Daily Planner

Date: _____

To do

Morning _____
_____
_____
_____
_____
_____
_____

Afternoon _____
_____
_____
_____
_____
_____
_____

Evening _____
_____
_____
_____
_____
_____
_____

Goals
_____
_____
_____
_____

Appointments
_____
_____

Call / Email
_____
_____

Meal Planner
_____
_____

Water Intake
○ ○ ○ ○
○ ○ ○ ○

Steps _____

Notes

"None is more impoverished than the one who has no gratitude. Gratitude is a currency that we can mint for ourselves, and spend without fear of bankruptcy." -- Fred De Witt Van Amburgh

_____
_____
_____
_____
_____
_____

Daily Planner

Date: _____

To do

Morning _____

_____

_____

_____

_____

_____

_____

_____

_____

Afternoon _____

_____

_____

_____

_____

_____

_____

Evening _____

_____

_____

_____

_____

_____

_____

Goals

_____

_____

_____

_____

_____

Appointments

_____

_____

Call / Email

_____

_____

Meal Planner

_____

_____

Water Intake

◯ ◯ ◯ ◯
◯ ◯ ◯ ◯

Steps _____

Notes

"Gratitude always comes into play; research shows that people are happier if they are grateful for the positive things in their lives, rather than worrying about what might be missing." -- Dan Buettner

_____

_____

_____

_____

_____

_____

Daily Planner

Date: _____

To do

Morning _____

_____
_____
_____
_____
_____
_____
_____

Afternoon _____

_____
_____
_____
_____
_____
_____
_____

Evening _____

_____
_____
_____
_____
_____
_____
_____

Goals

_____
_____
_____
_____

Appointments

_____
_____

Call / Email

_____
_____

Meal Planner

_____
_____

Water Intake

◯ ◯ ◯
◯ ◯ ◯

Steps _____

Notes

"The roots of all goodness lie in the soil of
appreciation for goodness." -- Dalai Lama

_____
_____
_____
_____
_____
_____
_____

Daily Planner

Date: _____

To do

Morning _____

_____
_____
_____
_____
_____
_____

Afternoon _____

_____
_____
_____
_____
_____
_____

Evening _____

_____
_____
_____
_____
_____
_____

Goals

_____
_____
_____
_____

Appointments

_____
_____

Call / Email

_____
_____

Meal Planner

_____
_____

Water Intake

○ ○ ○ ○
○ ○ ○ ○

Steps _____

Notes

"When I started counting my blessings, my whole life turned around." -- Willie Nelson

_____
_____
_____
_____
_____
_____
_____

workout log

Week

Date: _____ Time: _____ Week: _____

Workout Day: ① ② ③ ④ ⑤ ⑥ ⑦

Exercise	Reps	Set-1	Set-2	Set-3	Set-4	Set-5

Date: _____ Time: _____ Week: _____

Workout Day: ① ② ③ ④ ⑤ ⑥ ⑦

Exercise	Reps	Set-1	Set-2	Set-3	Set-4	Set-5

Weight

Body Fat

Chest

Right Arm

Left Arm

Waist

Hips

Right Leg

Left Leg

To Do List This Week

Day _____

Date & Month _____

No.	To Do	Yes/No
		☐ ☐
		☐ ☐
		☐ ☐
		☐ ☐
		☐ ☐
		☐ ☐
		☐ ☐
		☐ ☐
		☐ ☐
		☐ ☐
		☐ ☐
		☐ ☐
		☐ ☐
		☐ ☐
		☐ ☐
		☐ ☐
		☐ ☐
		☐ ☐
		☐ ☐

Notes _____

_____

_____

_____

Daily Planner

Date: _____

To do

Morning _____

_____

_____

_____

_____

_____

_____

_____

Afternoon _____

_____

_____

_____

_____

_____

_____

_____

Evening _____

_____

_____

_____

_____

_____

_____

Goals

_____

_____

_____

_____

Appointments

_____

_____

Call / Email

_____

_____

Meal Planner

_____

_____

Water Intake

◯ ◯ ◯ ◯
◯ ◯ ◯ ◯

Steps _____

Notes

"Appreciation can change a day, even change a life. Your willingness to put it into words is all that is necessary." -- Margaret Cousins

_____

_____

_____

_____

_____

_____

_____

Daily Planner

Date: _____

To do

Morning _____

_____

_____

_____

_____

_____

_____

_____

Afternoon _____

_____

_____

_____

_____

_____

_____

Evening _____

_____

_____

_____

_____

_____

_____

Goals

_____

_____

_____

_____

_____

Appointments

_____

_____

_____

Call / Email

_____

_____

_____

Meal Planner

_____

_____

Water Intake

◯ ◯ ◯ ◯
◯ ◯ ◯ ◯

Steps _____

Notes

"If you are really thankful, what do you do? You share." -- W. Clement Stone

_____

_____

_____

_____

_____

_____

_____

Daily Planner

Date: _____

To do

Morning _____

_____
_____
_____
_____
_____
_____
_____
_____

Afternoon _____

_____
_____
_____
_____
_____
_____

Evening _____

_____
_____
_____
_____
_____
_____
_____

Goals

_____
_____
_____
_____

Appointments

_____
_____

Call / Email

_____
_____

Meal Planner

_____
_____

Water Intake

◯ ◯ ◯
◯ ◯ ◯

Steps _____

Notes

"There are only two ways to live your life. One is as though nothing is a miracle. The other is as though everything is a miracle." -- Albert Einstein

_____
_____
_____
_____
_____
_____
_____

Daily Planner

Date: _____

To do

Morning _____

_____

_____

_____

_____

_____

_____

_____

_____

Afternoon _____

_____

_____

_____

_____

_____

_____

_____

Evening _____

_____

_____

_____

_____

_____

_____

Goals

_____

_____

_____

_____

_____

Appointments

_____

_____

_____

Call / Email

_____

_____

_____

Meal Planner

_____

_____

Water Intake

◯ ◯ ◯ ◯
◯ ◯ ◯ ◯

Steps _____

Notes

"Look at everything as though you were seeing it for the first or the last time, then your time on earth will be filled with glory." -- Betty Smith

_____

_____

_____

_____

_____

_____

_____

Daily Planner

Date: _____

To do

Morning _____

_____

_____

_____

_____

_____

_____

_____

Afternoon _____

_____

_____

_____

_____

_____

_____

Evening _____

_____

_____

_____

_____

_____

_____

_____

Goals

_____

_____

_____

_____

Appointments

_____

_____

_____

Call / Email

_____

_____

Meal Planner

_____

_____

Water Intake

◯ ◯ ◯ ◯
◯ ◯ ◯ ◯

Steps _____

Notes

"When you give and carry out acts of kindness, it's as though something inside your body responds and says, 'Yes, this is how I ought to feel."
Rabbi Harold Kushner

_____

_____

_____

_____

_____

_____

_____

Daily Planner

Date: _____

To do

Morning _____
_____
_____
_____

_____
_____
_____

Afternoon _____
_____
_____
_____
_____
_____
_____

Evening _____
_____
_____
_____
_____
_____
_____
_____

Goals
_____
_____
_____
_____
_____

Appointments
_____
_____
_____

Call / Email
_____
_____

Meal Planner
_____
_____
_____

Water Intake
◯ ◯ ◯ ◯
◯ ◯ ◯ ◯

Steps _____

Notes
"Not what we say about our blessings, but how we use them, is the true measure of our thanksgiving." -
- W.T. Purkiser
_____
_____
_____
_____
_____
_____
_____

Daily Planner

Date: _____

To do

Morning _____
_____
_____
_____
_____
_____
_____

Afternoon _____
_____
_____
_____
_____
_____
_____

Evening _____
_____
_____
_____
_____
_____
_____

Goals

_____
_____
_____
_____

Appointments

_____
_____
_____

Call / Email

_____
_____
_____

Meal Planner

_____
_____

Water Intake

◯ ◯ ◯ ◯
◯ ◯ ◯ ◯

Steps _____

Notes

"All across America, we gather this week with the people we love to give thanks to God for the blessings in our lives." -- President George W. Bush

_____
_____
_____
_____
_____
_____
_____

workout log

Week

Date: _____   Time: _____   Week: _____

Workout Day: ① ② ③ ④ ⑤ ⑥ ⑦

Exercise	Reps	Set-1	Set-2	Set-3	Set-4	Set-5

Date: _____   Time: _____   Week: _____

Workout Day: ① ② ③ ④ ⑤ ⑥ ⑦

Exercise	Reps	Set-1	Set-2	Set-3	Set-4	Set-5

Weight

Body Fat

Chest

Right Arm

Left Arm

Waist

Hips

Right Leg

Left Leg

To Do List This Week

Day _____

Date & Month _____

No.	To Do	Yes/No
_____	_____	☐ ☐
_____	_____	☐ ☐
_____	_____	☐ ☐
_____	_____	☐ ☐
_____	_____	☐ ☐
_____	_____	☐ ☐
_____	_____	☐ ☐
_____	_____	☐ ☐
_____	_____	☐ ☐
_____	_____	☐ ☐
_____	_____	☐ ☐
_____	_____	☐ ☐
_____	_____	☐ ☐
_____	_____	☐ ☐
_____	_____	☐ ☐
_____	_____	☐ ☐
_____	_____	☐ ☐
_____	_____	☐ ☐
_____	_____	☐ ☐
_____	_____	☐ ☐

Notes _____

_____

_____

Daily Planner

Date: _____

To do

Morning _____

_____

_____

_____

_____

_____

_____

_____

Afternoon _____

_____

_____

_____

_____

_____

_____

Evening _____

_____

_____

_____

_____

_____

_____

Goals

_____

_____

_____

_____

Appointments

_____

_____

Call / Email

_____

_____

Meal Planner

_____

_____

Water Intake

◯ ◯ ◯ ◯
◯ ◯ ◯ ◯

Steps _____

Notes

**Gratitude is one of the most powerful emotions that you can practice in your everyday life.
Former President George W. Bush**

_____

_____

_____

_____

_____

_____

_____

Date: _____

To do

Morning _____
_____
_____
_____
_____
_____
_____
_____

Afternoon _____
_____
_____
_____
_____
_____
_____

Evening _____
_____
_____
_____
_____
_____
_____
_____

Goals
_____
_____
_____
_____
_____
_____

Appointments
_____
_____
_____

Call / Email
_____
_____
_____

Meal Planner
_____
_____
_____

Water Intake
◯ ◯ ◯ ◯
◯ ◯ ◯ ◯

Steps _____

Notes
"Every great dream begins with a dreamer. Always remember, you have within you the strength, the patience, and the passion to reach for the stars to change the world." —Harriet Tubman
_____
_____
_____
_____
_____
_____
_____

Daily Planner

Date: _____

To do

Morning _____

_____
_____
_____
_____
_____
_____
_____

Afternoon _____

_____
_____
_____
_____
_____
_____
_____

Evening _____

_____
_____
_____
_____
_____
_____
_____

Goals

_____
_____
_____
_____
_____

Appointments

_____
_____
_____

Call / Email

_____
_____

Meal Planner

_____
_____

Water Intake

◯ ◯ ◯ ◯
◯ ◯ ◯ ◯

Steps _____

Notes

"Success is to be measured not so much by the position that one has reached in life as by the obstacles which he has overcome while trying to succeed." —Booker T. Washington

_____
_____
_____
_____
_____

Date: _____

To do

Morning _____

_____

_____

_____

_____

_____

_____

_____

Afternoon _____

_____

_____

_____

_____

_____

_____

Evening _____

_____

_____

_____

_____

_____

_____

Goals

_____

_____

_____

_____

_____

Appointments

_____

_____

Call / Email

_____

_____

Meal Planner

_____

_____

_____

Water Intake

○ ○ ○ ○
○ ○ ○ ○

Steps _____

Notes

"Change will not come if we wait for some other person, or if we wait for some other time. We are the ones we've been waiting for. We are the change that we seek." —Barack Obama

_____

_____

_____

_____

_____

_____

_____

Daily Planner

Date: _____

To do

Morning _____

_____
_____
_____
_____
_____
_____
_____

Afternoon _____

_____
_____
_____
_____
_____
_____
_____

Evening _____

_____
_____
_____
_____
_____
_____

Goals

_____
_____
_____
_____

Appointments

_____
_____

Call / Email

_____
_____

Meal Planner

_____
_____

Water Intake

◯ ◯ ◯ ◯
◯ ◯ ◯ ◯

Steps _____

Notes

"He who is not courageous enough to take risks will accomplish nothing in life." —Muhammad Ali

_____
_____
_____
_____
_____
_____
_____

Date: _____

To do

Morning _____

_____
_____
_____
_____
_____
_____
_____
_____

Afternoon _____

_____
_____
_____
_____
_____
_____

Evening _____

_____
_____
_____
_____
_____
_____

Goals

_____
_____
_____
_____
_____

Appointments

_____
_____

Call / Email

_____
_____

Meal Planner

_____
_____

Water Intake

Steps _____

Notes

"Won't it be wonderful when black history and Native American history and Jewish history and all of U.S. history is taught from one book. Just U.S. history." —Maya Angelou

_____
_____
_____
_____
_____
_____

Daily Planner

Date: _____

To do

Morning _____

_____

_____

_____

_____

_____

_____

_____

Afternoon _____

_____

_____

_____

_____

_____

_____

Evening _____

_____

_____

_____

_____

_____

_____

Goals

_____

_____

_____

_____

_____

Appointments

_____

_____

Call / Email

_____

_____

Meal Planner

_____

_____

Water Intake

◯ ◯ ◯ ◯
◯ ◯ ◯ ◯

Steps _____

Notes

"Did you know that the human voice is the only pure instrument? That it has notes no other instrument has? It's like being between the keys of a piano." —Nina Simone

_____

_____

_____

_____

_____

_____

MY MEETING NOTES

MEETING NAME & DATE -

ATTENDEES -

NEXT STEPS / DEADLINES -

MEETING NOTES -

_____

_____

_____

_____

_____

_____

_____

_____

_____

_____

_____

_____

_____

_____

_____

_____

_____

"Never be limited by other people's limited imaginations." —Dr. Mae Jemison

MY MEETING NOTES

MEETING NAME & DATE -

ATTENDEES -

NEXT STEPS / DEADLINES -

MEETING NOTES -

"You can't separate peace from freedom because no one can be at peace unless he has his freedom." —Malcolm X

MY MEETING NOTES

MEETING NAME & DATE -

ATTENDEES -

NEXT STEPS / DEADLINES -

MEETING NOTES -

"For I am my mother's daughter, and the drums of Africa still beat in my heart."
Mary McLeod Bethune

MY MEETING NOTES

MEETING NAME & DATE -

ATTENDEES -

NEXT STEPS / DEADLINES -

MEETING NOTES -

"I've missed more than 9,000 shots in my career. I've lost almost 300 games. 26 times, I've been trusted to take the game winning shot and missed. I've failed over and over and over again in my life. And that is why I succeed." —Michael Jordan

MY MEETING NOTES

MEETING NAME & DATE -

ATTENDEES -

NEXT STEPS / DEADLINES -

MEETING NOTES -

_____
_____
_____
_____
_____
_____
_____
_____
_____
_____
_____
_____
_____
_____
_____
_____
_____
_____
_____

"What's the world for if you can't make it up the way you want it?"—Toni Morrison

MY MEETING NOTES

MEETING NAME & DATE -

ATTENDEES -

NEXT STEPS / DEADLINES -

MEETING NOTES -

_____

_____

_____

_____

_____

_____

_____

_____

_____

_____

_____

_____

_____

_____

_____

_____

_____

_____

One of the hardest things in life to learn are which bridges to cross and which bridges to burn. Oprah Winfrey

MY MEETING NOTES

MEETING NAME & DATE -

ATTENDEES -

NEXT STEPS / DEADLINES -

MEETING NOTES -

"The soul that is within me no man can degrade." —Frederick Douglass

MY MEETING NOTES

MEETING NAME & DATE -

ATTENDEES -

NEXT STEPS / DEADLINES -

MEETING NOTES -

_____

_____

_____

_____

_____

_____

_____

_____

_____

_____

_____

_____

_____

_____

_____

_____

_____

_____

_____

"Just don't give up what you're trying to do. Where there is love and inspiration, I don't think you can go wrong." —Ella Fitzgerald

MY MEETING NOTES

MEETING NAME & DATE -

ATTENDEES -

NEXT STEPS / DEADLINES -

MEETING NOTES -

"I am America. I am the part you won't recognize. But get used to me. Black, confident, cocky;
my name, not yours; my religion, not yours; my goals, my own; get used to me."
Muhammad Ali

MY MEETING NOTES

MEETING NAME & DATE -

ATTENDEES -

NEXT STEPS / DEADLINES -

MEETING NOTES -

_____

_____

_____

_____

_____

_____

_____

_____

_____

_____

_____

_____

_____

_____

_____

_____

_____

"The one thing I feel is lacking in Hollywood today is an understanding of the beauty, the power, the sexuality, the uniqueness, the humor of being a regular Black woman."
Viola Davis

MY MEETING NOTES

MEETING NAME & DATE -

ATTENDEES -

NEXT STEPS / DEADLINES -

MEETING NOTES -

"Impossible is just a big word thrown around by small men who find it easier to live in the world they've been given than to explore the power they have to change it. Impossible is not a fact. It's an opinion. Impossible is not a declaration. It's a dare. Impossible is potential. Impossible is temporary. Impossible is nothing." —Muhammad Ali

MY MEETING NOTES

MEETING NAME & DATE -

ATTENDEES -

NEXT STEPS / DEADLINES -

MEETING NOTES -

"It was when I realized I needed to stop trying to be somebody else and be myself, I actually started to own, accept, and love what I had." —Tracee Ellis Ross

MONTHLY REVIEW

THIS MONTH I ACHIEVED

_____

_____

_____

_____

_____

_____

_____

_____

WHAT WORKED

_____

_____

_____

WHAT DIDN'T WORK

_____

_____

_____

DO MORE OF	DO LESS OF

MONTHLY REVIEW

THIS MONTH I ACHIEVED

_____
_____
_____
_____
_____
_____
_____
_____
_____
_____

WHAT WORKED

_____
_____
_____
_____

WHAT DIDN'T WORK

_____
_____
_____
_____

DO MORE OF

DO LESS OF

JANUARY

MON
LEGS

Stretching and warm-up
25 Squats
25 Sumo Squats
Repeat above March in place for 20 sec
Stretch muscles
Relax

TUES
ABS

Stretching and warm-up
20 Standing Oblique Twists
30-second Floor Plank
Repeat above
March in place for 20 seconds
Stretch muscles
Relax

WED
ARMS

Stretching and warm-up
25 Push-ups
20 Wall Tricep Pushes
Repeat above
March in place for 20
seconds
Stretch muscles
Relax

THURS
CARDIO

Stretching and warm-up
50 Jumping Jacks
30-second Sprint in place
Repeat above
March in place for 20
seconds
Stretch muscles
Relax

FRI
COMBO

Stretching and warm-up
10 Squats & 10 Sumo
Squats
10 Standing Oblique Twists
March in place for 20
seconds
20 Push-ups
25 Jumping Jacks
March in place for 20
seconds
Stretch muscles
Relax

SAT
YOUR PICK

Choose from Day 1-4
to work on your chosen area:
Legs
Abs
Arms or
Cardio

SUN
REST

Take a break!
You deserve it.

workout log

Week

Date : Time : Week :

Workout Day : 1 2 3 4 5 6 7

Exercise	Reps	Set -1	Set -2	Set -3	Set -4	Set -5

Date : Time : Week :

Workout Day : 1 2 3 4 5 6 7

Exercise	Reps	Set -1	Set -2	Set -3	Set -4	Set -5

Weight

Body Fat

Chest

Right Arm

Left Arm

Waist

Hips

Right Leg

Left Leg

THIS MONTH'S LIST
Month: January Year: _____

Potential Items to Plan/Schedule

District Board Mtg
District Principal Mtg
Vertical Team Mtg
Parent Conferences
LPACs/ELLs/ARDs
Progress Report/Report Cards
Master Schedule Review
Team Leader/Dept. Chair Mtg
Campus Admin Mtg
Professional Learning Committee (PLC) Mtg
Shared Decision Making Council (SDMC) Mtg
Athletic Event Admin Coverage Schedule
Teachers I need to meet with (observe/walkthrough)

Potential Assessments

Circle Pre-K
EOC for High School
Dyslexia Screener
Renaissance Screener Math/Alg1/Eng I/II
State Assessment Practice
Benchmark/Running Records
National Assessment of Educational Progress (NAEP)
High Frequency Word Exam (Gr. 1 & 2)

Additions:

Senior Ranking Roster Development and Ceremony
Senior Trip/Activity
Senior Picture Day

_____
_____
_____
_____
_____
_____
_____

MONTHLY PLANNER
MONTH: _____

MONDAY	TUESDAY	WEDNESDAY	THURSDAY	FRIDAY	SATURDAY	SUNDAY

PRIORITY

To Do List This Week

Day _____

Date & Month _____

No.	To Do	Yes/No	
___	_____	☐	☐
___	_____	☐	☐
___	_____	☐	☐
___	_____	☐	☐
___	_____	☐	☐
___	_____	☐	☐
___	_____	☐	☐
___	_____	☐	☐
___	_____	☐	☐
___	_____	☐	☐
___	_____	☐	☐
___	_____	☐	☐
___	_____	☐	☐
___	_____	☐	☐
___	_____	☐	☐
___	_____	☐	☐
___	_____	☐	☐
___	_____	☐	☐
___	_____	☐	☐
___	_____	☐	☐

Notes _____

_____

_____

_____

Daily Planner

Date: _____

To do

Morning _____

_____

_____

_____

_____

_____

_____

Afternoon _____

_____

_____

_____

_____

_____

_____

_____

Evening _____

_____

_____

_____

_____

_____

_____

Goals

_____

_____

_____

_____

_____

Appointments

_____

_____

Call / Email

_____

_____

Meal Planner

_____

_____

Water Intake

○ ○ ○ ○
○ ○ ○ ○

Steps _____

Notes

Booker T. Washington, author and advisor to U.S. presidents: "Excellence is to do a common thing in an uncommon way."

_____

_____

_____

_____

_____

_____

_____

Daily Planner

Date: _____

To do

Morning _____

_____

_____

_____

_____

_____

_____

_____

Afternoon _____

_____

_____

_____

_____

_____

_____

Evening _____

_____

_____

_____

_____

_____

Goals

_____

_____

_____

_____

_____

Appointments

_____

_____

Call / Email

_____

_____

Meal Planner

_____

_____

Water Intake

○ ○ ○ ○
○ ○ ○ ○

Steps _____

Notes

Aristotle: "Excellence is an art won by training and habituation. We do not act rightly because we have virtue or excellence, but we rather have those because we have acted rightly. We are what we repeatedly do. Excellence, then, is not an act but a habit."

_____

_____

_____

_____

_____

Daily Planner

Date: _____

To do

Morning _____
_____
_____
_____
_____
_____
_____
_____

Afternoon _____
_____
_____
_____
_____
_____
_____
_____

Evening _____
_____
_____
_____
_____
_____
_____
_____

Goals
_____
_____
_____
_____
_____

Appointments
_____
_____

Call / Email
_____
_____

Meal Planner
_____
_____

Water Intake
○ ○ ○
○ ○ ○

Steps _____

Notes
Barack Obama: "We need to internalize this idea of excellence. Not many folks spend a lot of time trying to be excellent."
_____
_____
_____
_____
_____
_____
_____

Daily Planner

Date: _____

To do

Morning _____

_____

_____

_____

_____

_____

_____

_____

Afternoon _____

_____

_____

_____

_____

_____

_____

Evening _____

_____

_____

_____

_____

_____

_____

Goals

_____

_____

_____

_____

_____

Appointments

_____

_____

Call / Email

_____

_____

Meal Planner

_____

_____

Water Intake

◯ ◯ ◯ ◯
◯ ◯ ◯ ◯

Steps _____

Notes

Brene Brown, author and researcher: "To me, a leader is someone who holds her- or himself accountable for finding potential in people and processes."

_____

_____

_____

_____

_____

_____

_____

_____

Daily Planner

Date: _____

To do

Morning _____

_____

_____

_____

_____

_____

_____

Afternoon _____

_____

_____

_____

_____

_____

_____

Evening _____

_____

_____

_____

_____

_____

_____

Goals

_____

_____

_____

_____

Appointments

_____

_____

_____

Call / Email

_____

_____

Meal Planner

_____

_____

Water Intake

○ ○ ○ ○
○ ○ ○ ○

Steps _____

Notes

Cornel West, philosopher and author: "You can't lead the people if you don't love the people. You can't save the people if you don't serve the people."

_____

_____

_____

_____

_____

_____

_____

Daily Planner

Date: _____

To do

Morning _____

_____
_____
_____
_____
_____
_____
_____

Afternoon _____

_____
_____
_____
_____
_____
_____

Evening _____

_____
_____
_____
_____
_____
_____
_____

Goals

_____
_____
_____
_____

Appointments

_____
_____
_____

Call / Email

_____
_____

Meal Planner

_____
_____

Water Intake

○ ○ ○ ○
○ ○ ○ ○

Steps _____

Notes

**Albert Einstein, German-born theoretical physicist:
"We cannot solve our problems with the same
thinking we used when we created them."**

_____
_____
_____
_____
_____
_____

Daily Planner

Date: _____

To do

Morning _____
_____
_____
_____
_____
_____
_____
_____

Afternoon _____
_____
_____
_____
_____
_____
_____

Evening _____
_____
_____
_____
_____
_____
_____

Goals

_____
_____
_____
_____
_____

Appointments

_____
_____

Call / Email

_____
_____

Meal Planner

_____
_____

Water Intake

◯ ◯ ◯ ◯
◯ ◯ ◯ ◯

Steps _____

Notes

Elena Kagan, Associate Justice of the Supreme Court of the United States: "I've led a school whose faculty and students examine and discuss and debate every aspect of our law and legal system. And what I've learned most is that no one has a monopoly on truth or wisdom. I've learned that we make progress by listening to each other, across every apparent political or ideological divide."

_____
_____
_____

workout log

Week

Date: [   ]   Time: [   ]   Week: [   ]

Workout Day: ① ② ③ ④ ⑤ ⑥ ⑦

Exercise	Reps	Set-1	Set-2	Set-3	Set-4	Set-5

Date: [   ]   Time: [   ]   Week: [   ]

Workout Day: ① ② ③ ④ ⑤ ⑥ ⑦

Exercise	Reps	Set-1	Set-2	Set-3	Set-4	Set-5

Weight

Body Fat

Chest

Right Arm

Left Arm

Waist

Hips

Right Leg

Left Leg

To Do List This Week

Day _____

Date & Month _____

No.	To Do	Yes/No	
_____	_____	☐	☐
_____	_____	☐	☐
_____	_____	☐	☐
_____	_____	☐	☐
_____	_____	☐	☐
_____	_____	☐	☐
_____	_____	☐	☐
_____	_____	☐	☐
_____	_____	☐	☐
_____	_____	☐	☐
_____	_____	☐	☐
_____	_____	☐	☐
_____	_____	☐	☐
_____	_____	☐	☐
_____	_____	☐	☐
_____	_____	☐	☐
_____	_____	☐	☐
_____	_____	☐	☐
_____	_____	☐	☐
_____	_____	☐	☐

Notes _____

_____

_____

_____

Daily Planner

Date: _____

To do

Morning _____

_____

_____

_____

_____

_____

_____

_____

Afternoon _____

_____

_____

_____

_____

_____

_____

Evening _____

_____

_____

_____

_____

_____

_____

Goals

_____

_____

_____

_____

_____

Appointments

_____

_____

Call / Email

_____

_____

Meal Planner

_____

_____

Water Intake

○ ○ ○ ○
○ ○ ○ ○

Steps _____

Notes

Laura Ingalls Wilder, author of the "Little House on the Prairie" series: "The trouble with organizing a thing is that pretty soon folks get to paying more attention to the organization than to what they're organized for."

_____

_____

_____

_____

_____

_____

Daily Planner

Date: _____

To do

Morning _____

_____

_____

_____

_____

_____

_____

_____

Afternoon _____

_____

_____

_____

_____

_____

_____

Evening _____

_____

_____

_____

_____

_____

_____

Goals

_____

_____

_____

_____

_____

Appointments

_____

_____

_____

Call / Email

_____

_____

_____

Meal Planner

_____

_____

Water Intake

○ ○ ○ ○
○ ○ ○ ○

Steps _____

Notes

Albert Einstein: "If you can't explain it simply, you don't understand it well enough."

_____

_____

_____

_____

_____

_____

_____

Daily Planner

Date: _____

To do

Morning _____

_____

_____

_____

_____

_____

_____

_____

_____

Afternoon _____

_____

_____

_____

_____

_____

_____

Evening _____

_____

_____

_____

_____

_____

_____

Goals

_____

_____

_____

_____

_____

Appointments

_____

_____

_____

Call / Email

_____

_____

_____

Meal Planner

_____

_____

Water Intake

◯ ◯ ◯ ◯
◯ ◯ ◯ ◯

Steps _____

Notes

**Chris Dede, education researcher and innovator:
"There is no single best way to teach because there
is no single best way to learn."**

_____

_____

_____

_____

_____

_____

_____

Date: _____

To do

Morning _____
_____
_____
_____
_____
_____
_____

Afternoon _____
_____
_____
_____
_____
_____
_____

Evening _____
_____
_____
_____
_____
_____
_____

Goals
_____
_____
_____
_____

Appointments
_____
_____

Call / Email
_____
_____

Meal Planner
_____
_____

Water Intake
◯ ◯ ◯ ◯
◯ ◯ ◯ ◯

Steps _____

Notes

Septima Poinsette Clark, civil rights activist: "I believe unconditionally in the ability of people to respond when they are told the truth. We need to be taught to study rather than believe, to inquire rather than to affirm."

_____
_____
_____
_____

Daily Planner

Date: _____

To do

Morning _____

_____

_____

_____

_____

_____

_____

_____

Afternoon _____

_____

_____

_____

_____

_____

_____

_____

Evening _____

_____

_____

_____

_____

_____

_____

_____

Goals

_____

_____

_____

_____

_____

Appointments

_____

_____

_____

Call / Email

_____

_____

_____

Meal Planner

_____

_____

Water Intake

◯ ◯ ◯ ◯
◯ ◯ ◯ ◯

Steps _____

Notes

Maya Angelou, poet and civil rights activist: "I've learned that people will forget what you said, people will forget what you did, but people will never forget how you made them feel."

_____

_____

_____

_____

_____

_____

_____

Daily Planner

Date: _____

To do

Morning _____

_____

_____

_____

_____

_____

_____

Afternoon _____

_____

_____

_____

_____

_____

_____

Evening _____

_____

_____

_____

_____

_____

Goals

_____

_____

_____

_____

_____

Appointments

_____

_____

Call / Email

_____

_____

Meal Planner

_____

_____

Water Intake

◯ ◯ ◯ ◯
◯ ◯ ◯ ◯

Steps _____

Notes

Maria Montessori, Italian physician best known for the education philosophy that bears her name: "One test of the correctness of educational procedure is the happiness of the child."

_____

_____

_____

_____

_____

_____

Daily Planner

Date: _____

To do

Morning _____

_____
_____
_____
_____
_____
_____
_____

Afternoon _____

_____
_____
_____
_____
_____
_____

Evening _____

_____
_____
_____
_____
_____
_____

Goals

_____
_____
_____
_____
_____

Appointments

_____
_____
_____

Call / Email

_____
_____
_____

Meal Planner

_____
_____

Water Intake

○ ○ ○ ○
○ ○ ○ ○

Steps _____

Notes

Jaime Escalante, calculus teacher whose life inspired the film "Stand and Deliver": "If we expect kids to be losers they will be losers; if we expect them to be winners they will be winners. They rise, or fall, to the level of the expectations of those around them, especially their parents and their teachers."

_____
_____
_____
_____
_____

workout log

Week

Date: _____ Time: _____ Week: _____

Workout Day: ① ② ③ ④ ⑤ ⑥ ⑦

Exercise	Reps	Set-1	Set-2	Set-3	Set-4	Set-5

Date: _____ Time: _____ Week: _____

Workout Day: ① ② ③ ④ ⑤ ⑥ ⑦

Exercise	Reps	Set-1	Set-2	Set-3	Set-4	Set-5

Weight

Body Fat

Chest

Right Arm

Left Arm

Waist

Hips

Right Leg

Left Leg

To Do List This Week

Day _____

Date & Month _____

No.	To Do	Yes/No
___	_____	☐ ☐
___	_____	☐ ☐
___	_____	☐ ☐
___	_____	☐ ☐
___	_____	☐ ☐
___	_____	☐ ☐
___	_____	☐ ☐
___	_____	☐ ☐
___	_____	☐ ☐
___	_____	☐ ☐
___	_____	☐ ☐
___	_____	☐ ☐
___	_____	☐ ☐
___	_____	☐ ☐
___	_____	☐ ☐
___	_____	☐ ☐
___	_____	☐ ☐
___	_____	☐ ☐
___	_____	☐ ☐
___	_____	☐ ☐

Notes _____

_____

_____

_____

Daily Planner

Date: _____

To do

Morning _____

_____

_____

_____

_____

_____

_____

_____

_____

Afternoon _____

_____

_____

_____

_____

_____

_____

Evening _____

_____

_____

_____

_____

_____

_____

Goals

_____

_____

_____

_____

_____

Appointments

_____

_____

Call / Email

_____

_____

Meal Planner

_____

_____

Water Intake

◯ ◯ ◯
◯ ◯ ◯

Steps _____

Notes

Mary McLeod Bethune, civil rights activist and co-founder of Bethune-Cookman University: "We have a powerful potential in our youth, and we must have the courage to change old ideas and practices so that we may direct their power toward good ends."

_____

_____

_____

_____

_____

Daily Planner

Date: _____

To do

Morning _____
_____
_____
_____
_____
_____
_____
_____

Afternoon _____
_____
_____
_____
_____
_____
_____
_____

Evening _____
_____
_____
_____
_____
_____
_____
_____

Goals

_____
_____
_____
_____

Appointments

_____
_____

Call / Email

_____
_____

Meal Planner

_____
_____

Water Intake

○ ○ ○ ○
○ ○ ○ ○

Steps _____

Notes

Dorothy Height, civil rights and women's rights activist: "You never teach a subject, you always teach a child. You teach children in a way that they will learn, and then things will fall in place for them."

_____
_____
_____
_____
_____

Daily Planner

Date: _____

To do

Morning _____

_____

_____

_____

_____

_____

_____

_____

Afternoon _____

_____

_____

_____

_____

_____

_____

Evening _____

_____

_____

_____

_____

_____

_____

Goals

_____

_____

_____

_____

Appointments

_____

_____

Call / Email

_____

_____

Meal Planner

_____

_____

Water Intake

○ ○ ○ ○
○ ○ ○ ○

Steps _____

Notes

Stephen Hawking, physicist and author:
"Intelligence is the ability to adapt to change."

_____

_____

_____

_____

_____

_____

_____

Daily Planner

Date: _____

To do

Morning _____

_____
_____
_____
_____
_____
_____
_____

Afternoon _____

_____
_____
_____
_____
_____
_____
_____

Evening _____

_____
_____
_____
_____
_____
_____

Goals

_____
_____
_____
_____
_____

Appointments

_____
_____

Call / Email

_____
_____

Meal Planner

_____
_____

Water Intake

◯ ◯ ◯ ◯
◯ ◯ ◯ ◯

Steps _____

Notes

Temple Grandin, animal science and autism education expert: "The world needs all types of minds."

_____
_____
_____
_____
_____
_____
_____
_____

Daily Planner

Date: _____

To do

Morning _____

_____
_____
_____
_____
_____
_____
_____

Afternoon _____

_____
_____
_____
_____
_____
_____
_____

Evening _____

_____
_____
_____
_____
_____
_____

Goals

_____
_____
_____
_____
_____

Appointments

_____
_____

Call / Email

_____
_____

Meal Planner

_____
_____

Water Intake

◯ ◯ ◯
◯ ◯ ◯

Steps _____

Notes

Albert Einstein: "The true sign of intelligence is not knowledge but imagination."

_____
_____
_____
_____
_____
_____
_____

Daily Planner

Date: _____

To do

Morning _____

_____

_____

_____

_____

_____

_____

_____

Afternoon _____

_____

_____

_____

_____

_____

_____

Evening _____

_____

_____

_____

_____

_____

_____

Goals

_____

_____

_____

_____

_____

Appointments

_____

_____

_____

Call / Email

_____

_____

_____

Meal Planner

_____

_____

Water Intake

◯ ◯ ◯ ◯
◯ ◯ ◯ ◯

Steps _____

Notes

Fred Rogers, host of "Mister Rogers Neighborhood,": "Play is often talked about as if it were a relief from serious learning. But for children play is serious learning. Play is really the work of childhood."

_____

_____

_____

_____

_____

Daily Planner

Date: _____

To do

Morning _____

_____

_____

_____

_____

_____

_____

_____

Afternoon _____

_____

_____

_____

_____

_____

_____

_____

Evening _____

_____

_____

_____

_____

_____

_____

_____

Goals

_____

_____

_____

_____

_____

Appointments

_____

_____

_____

Call / Email

_____

_____

Meal Planner

_____

_____

_____

Water Intake

◯ ◯ ◯ ◯
◯ ◯ ◯ ◯

Steps _____

Notes

The function of education is to teach one to think intensively and to think critically. Intelligence plus character - that is the goal of true education. Martin Luther King, Jr.

_____

_____

_____

_____

_____

_____

workout log

Week

Date : _____   Time : _____   Week : _____

Workout Day : ① ② ③ ④ ⑤ ⑥ ⑦

Exercise	Reps	Set -1	Set -2	Set -3	Set -4	Set -5

Date : _____   Time : _____   Week : _____

Workout Day : ① ② ③ ④ ⑤ ⑥ ⑦

Exercise	Reps	Set -1	Set -2	Set -3	Set -4	Set -5

Weight

Body Fat

Chest

Right Arm

Left Arm

Waist

Hips

Right Leg

Left Leg

To Do List This Week

Day ——————

Date & Month ——————

No.	To Do	Yes/No
_____	_____	☐ ☐
_____	_____	☐ ☐
_____	_____	☐ ☐
_____	_____	☐ ☐
_____	_____	☐ ☐
_____	_____	☐ ☐
_____	_____	☐ ☐
_____	_____	☐ ☐
_____	_____	☐ ☐
_____	_____	☐ ☐
_____	_____	☐ ☐
_____	_____	☐ ☐
_____	_____	☐ ☐
_____	_____	☐ ☐
_____	_____	☐ ☐
_____	_____	☐ ☐
_____	_____	☐ ☐
_____	_____	☐ ☐
_____	_____	☐ ☐
_____	_____	☐ ☐

Notes _____

_____

_____

_____

Daily Planner

Date: _____

To do

Morning _____

_____

_____

_____

_____

_____

_____

_____

Afternoon _____

_____

_____

_____

_____

_____

_____

Evening _____

_____

_____

_____

_____

_____

_____

Goals

_____

_____

_____

_____

_____

Appointments

_____

_____

Call / Email

_____

_____

Meal Planner

_____

_____

Water Intake

◯ ◯ ◯ ◯
◯ ◯ ◯ ◯

Steps _____

Notes

Education is the most powerful weapon, which you can use to change the world. Nelson Mandela

_____

_____

_____

_____

_____

_____

_____

Daily Planner

Date: _____

To do

Morning _____

_____

_____

_____

_____

_____

_____

_____

Afternoon _____

_____

_____

_____

_____

_____

_____

_____

Evening _____

_____

_____

_____

_____

_____

_____

_____

Goals

_____

_____

_____

_____

Appointments

_____

_____

Call / Email

_____

_____

Meal Planner

_____

_____

Water Intake

○ ○ ○ ○
○ ○ ○ ○

Steps _____

Notes

Education is not preparation for life; education is life itself. John Dewey

_____

_____

_____

_____

_____

_____

_____

Daily Planner

Date: _____

To do

Morning _____

_____

_____

_____

_____

_____

_____

_____

Afternoon _____

_____

_____

_____

_____

_____

_____

_____

Evening _____

_____

_____

_____

_____

_____

_____

Goals

_____

_____

_____

_____

_____

Appointments

_____

_____

_____

Call / Email

_____

_____

_____

Meal Planner

_____

_____

Water Intake

○ ○ ○ ○
○ ○ ○ ○

Steps _____

Notes

The whole purpose of education is to turn mirrors into windows. Sydney J. Harris

_____

_____

_____

_____

_____

_____

_____

Daily Planner

Date: _____

To do

_____

Morning _____

_____

_____

_____

_____

_____

_____

_____

Afternoon _____

_____

_____

_____

_____

_____

_____

_____

Evening _____

_____

_____

_____

_____

_____

_____

Goals

_____

_____

_____

_____

_____

Appointments

_____

_____

_____

Call / Email

_____

_____

_____

Meal Planner

_____

_____

Water Intake

◯ ◯ ◯ ◯
◯ ◯ ◯ ◯

Steps _____

Notes

"It was when I realized I needed to stop trying to be somebody else and be myself, I actually started to own, accept, and love what I had."
Tracee Ellis Ross

_____

_____

_____

_____

_____

_____

_____

Daily Planner

Date: _____

To do

Morning _____

_____

_____

_____

_____

_____

_____

Afternoon _____

_____

_____

_____

_____

_____

_____

Evening _____

_____

_____

_____

_____

_____

Goals

_____

_____

_____

_____

_____

Appointments

_____

_____

Call / Email

_____

_____

Meal Planner

_____

_____

Water Intake

◯ ◯ ◯
◯ ◯ ◯

Steps _____

Notes

"The ultimate measure of a man is not where he stands in moments of comfort and convenience, but where he stands at times of challenge and controversy." —Martin Luther King, Jr.

_____

_____

_____

_____

_____

Daily Planner

Date: _____

To do

Morning _____
_____
_____
_____
_____
_____
_____
_____

Afternoon _____
_____
_____
_____
_____
_____
_____

Evening _____
_____
_____
_____
_____
_____
_____

Goals
_____
_____
_____
_____

Appointments
_____
_____

Call / Email
_____
_____

Meal Planner
_____
_____

Water Intake
◯ ◯ ◯ ◯
◯ ◯ ◯ ◯

Steps _____

Notes
"Your willingness to look at your darkness is what empowers you to change." —Iyanla Vanzant
_____
_____
_____
_____
_____
_____
_____

Daily Planner

Date: _____

To do

Morning _____
_____
_____
_____
_____
_____
_____

Afternoon _____
_____
_____
_____
_____
_____
_____

Evening _____
_____
_____
_____
_____
_____
_____

Goals

_____
_____
_____
_____
_____

Appointments

_____
_____

Call / Email

_____
_____

Meal Planner

_____
_____

Water Intake

○ ○ ○ ○
○ ○ ○ ○

Steps _____

Notes

"True peace is not merely the absence of tension; it is the presence of justice." —Martin Luther King Jr.

_____
_____
_____
_____
_____
_____
_____

MY MEETING NOTES

MEETING NAME & DATE -

ATTENDEES -

NEXT STEPS / DEADLINES -

MEETING NOTES -

_____
_____
_____
_____
_____
_____
_____
_____
_____
_____
_____
_____
_____
_____
_____
_____
_____
_____
_____

"When we're talking about diversity, it's not a box to check. It is a reality that should be deeply felt and held and valued by all of us." —Ava DuVernay

MY MEETING NOTES

MEETING NAME & DATE -

ATTENDEES -

NEXT STEPS / DEADLINES -

MEETING NOTES -

"I always believed that when you follow your heart or your gut, when you really follow the things that feel great to you, you can never lose, because settling is the worst feeling in the world." —Rihanna

MY MEETING NOTES

MEETING NAME & DATE -

ATTENDEES -

NEXT STEPS / DEADLINES -

MEETING NOTES -

"Challenges are gifts that force us to search for a new center of gravity. Don't fight them. Just find a new way to stand." —Oprah Winfrey

MY MEETING NOTES

MEETING NAME & DATE -

ATTENDEES -

NEXT STEPS / DEADLINES -

MEETING NOTES -

"Belief in oneself and knowing who you are—I mean, that's the foundation for everything great." —Jay-Z

MY MEETING NOTES

MEETING NAME & DATE -

ATTENDEES -

NEXT STEPS / DEADLINES -

MEETING NOTES -

_____

_____

_____

_____

_____

_____

_____

_____

_____

_____

_____

_____

_____

_____

_____

_____

_____

_____

_____

"Go to work in the morn of a new creation...until you have...reached the height of self-progress, and from that pinnacle bestow upon the world a civilization of your own." —Marcus Garvey

MY MEETING NOTES

MEETING NAME & DATE -

ATTENDEES -

NEXT STEPS / DEADLINES -

MEETING NOTES -

"It's not the load that breaks you down; it's the way you carry it." —Lena Horne

MY MEETING NOTES

MEETING NAME & DATE -

ATTENDEES -

NEXT STEPS / DEADLINES -

MEETING NOTES -

"There have been so many people who have said to me, 'You can't do that,' but I've had an innate belief that they were wrong. Be unwavering and relentless in your approach."
Halle Berry

MY MEETING NOTES

MEETING NAME & DATE -

ATTENDEES -

NEXT STEPS / DEADLINES -

MEETING NOTES -

"We should emphasize not Negro History, but the Negro in history. What we need is not a history of selected races or nations, but the history of the world void of national bias, race hate, and religious prejudice." —Carter Woodson

MY MEETING NOTES

MEETING NAME & DATE -

ATTENDEES -

NEXT STEPS / DEADLINES -

MEETING NOTES -

"For to be free is not merely to cast off one's chains, but to live in a way that respects and enhances the freedom of others." —Nelson Mandela

MY MEETING NOTES

MEETING NAME & DATE -

ATTENDEES -

NEXT STEPS / DEADLINES -

MEETING NOTES -

"The thing about Black history is that the truth is so much more complex than anything you could make up." —Henry Louis Gates

MY MEETING NOTES

MEETING NAME & DATE -

ATTENDEES -

NEXT STEPS / DEADLINES -

MEETING NOTES -

_____
_____
_____
_____
_____
_____
_____
_____
_____
_____
_____
_____
_____
_____
_____
_____
_____
_____
_____
_____
_____
_____

"Life has two rules: number 1, never quit! Number 2, always remember rule number one."
Duke Ellington

MY MEETING NOTES

MEETING NAME & DATE -

ATTENDEES -

NEXT STEPS / DEADLINES -

MEETING NOTES -

"You don't make progress by standing on the sidelines, whimpering and complaining. You make progress by implementing ideas." —Shirley Chisholm

MONTHLY REVIEW

THIS MONTH I ACHIEVED

_____

_____

_____

_____

_____

_____

_____

_____

WHAT WORKED

_____

_____

_____

WHAT DIDN'T WORK

_____

_____

_____

DO MORE OF	DO LESS OF

MONTHLY REVIEW

THIS MONTH I ACHIEVED

_____

_____

_____

_____

_____

_____

_____

_____

_____

WHAT WORKED

_____

_____

_____

_____

WHAT DIDN'T WORK

_____

_____

_____

DO MORE OF	DO LESS OF

FEBRUARY

MON
LEGS

Stretching and warm-up
25 Squats
25 Sumo Squats
Repeat above March in place for 20 sec
Stretch muscles
Relax

TUES
ABS

Stretching and warm-up
20 Standing Oblique Twists
30-second Floor Plank
Repeat above
March in place for 20 seconds
Stretch muscles
Relax

WED
ARMS

Stretching and warm-up
25 Push-ups
20 Wall Tricep Pushes
Repeat above
March in place for 20 seconds
Stretch muscles
Relax

THURS
CARDIO

Stretching and warm-up
50 Jumping Jacks
30-second Sprint in place
Repeat above
March in place for 20 seconds
Stretch muscles
Relax

FRI
COMBO

Stretching and warm-up
10 Squats & 10 Sumo
Squats
10 Standing Oblique Twists
March in place for 20
seconds
20 Push-ups
25 Jumping Jacks
March in place for 20
seconds
Stretch muscles
Relax

SAT
YOUR PICK

Choose from Day 1-4
to work on your chosen area:
Legs
Abs
Arms or
Cardio

SUN
REST

Take a break!
You deserve it.

workout log

Week

Date :   Time :   Week :

Workout Day : ① ② ③ ④ ⑤ ⑥ ⑦

Exercise	Reps	Set -1	Set -2	Set -3	Set -4	Set -5

Date :   Time :   Week :

Workout Day : ① ② ③ ④ ⑤ ⑥ ⑦

Exercise	Reps	Set -1	Set -2	Set -3	Set -4	Set -5

Weight

Body Fat

Chest

Right Arm

Left Arm

Waist

Hips

Right Leg

Left Leg

Month: February Year: _____

Potential Items to Plan/Schedule
District Board Mtg
District Principal Mtg
Vertical Team Mtg
Parent Conferences
LPACs/ELLs/ARDs
Progress Reports/Report Cards
Master Schedule Review
Team Leader/Dept. Chair Mtg
Campus Admin Mtg
Professional Learning Community (PLC)
Athletic Event Admin Coverage Schedule
Teachers I need to meet with (observe/walkthrough)

Potential Assessments
State Level Field Test
Credit By Exam Option
ASVAB
District Level Snapshot/State Released

Additions
Graduation Planning for High Schools
Senior Week Activities Planning for High Schools
Prom Planning for High School
Promotion Planning Activity
School Field Day Activity Planning

_____
_____
_____
_____
_____
_____

MONTHLY PLANNER
MONTH: _____

MONDAY	TUESDAY	WEDNESDAY	THURSDAY	FRIDAY	SATURDAY	SUNDAY

PRIORITY

To Do List This Week

Day _____

Date & Month _____

No.	To Do	Yes/No
___	_____	☐ ☐
___	_____	☐ ☐
___	_____	☐ ☐
___	_____	☐ ☐
___	_____	☐ ☐
___	_____	☐ ☐
___	_____	☐ ☐
___	_____	☐ ☐
___	_____	☐ ☐
___	_____	☐ ☐
___	_____	☐ ☐
___	_____	☐ ☐
___	_____	☐ ☐
___	_____	☐ ☐
___	_____	☐ ☐
___	_____	☐ ☐
___	_____	☐ ☐
___	_____	☐ ☐
___	_____	☐ ☐
___	_____	☐ ☐

Notes _____

_____

_____

_____

Daily Planner

Date: _____

To do

Morning _____

_____

_____

_____

_____

_____

_____

_____

Afternoon _____

_____

_____

_____

_____

_____

_____

_____

Evening _____

_____

_____

_____

_____

_____

_____

_____

Goals

_____

_____

_____

_____

Appointments

_____

_____

Call / Email

_____

_____

Meal Planner

_____

_____

Water Intake

◯ ◯ ◯ ◯
◯ ◯ ◯ ◯

Steps _____

Notes

The only person who is educated is the one who has learned how to learn and change. Carl Rogers

_____

_____

_____

_____

_____

_____

_____

Daily Planner

Date: _____

To do

Morning _____

_____

_____

_____

_____

_____

_____

Afternoon _____

_____

_____

_____

_____

_____

_____

Evening _____

_____

_____

_____

_____

_____

_____

Goals

_____

_____

_____

_____

_____

Appointments

_____

_____

Call / Email

_____

_____

Meal Planner

_____

_____

Water Intake

◯ ◯ ◯
◯ ◯ ◯

Steps _____

Notes

An investment in knowledge pays the best interest.
Benjamin Franklin

_____

_____

_____

_____

_____

_____

_____

Daily Planner

Date: _____

To do

Morning _____
_____
_____
_____
_____
_____
_____
_____

Afternoon _____
_____
_____
_____
_____
_____
_____

Evening _____
_____
_____
_____
_____
_____
_____
_____

Goals

_____
_____
_____
_____
_____

Appointments

_____
_____

Call / Email

_____
_____

Meal Planner

_____
_____

Water Intake

○ ○ ○ ○
○ ○ ○ ○

Steps _____

Notes

"When we talk about 21st century pedagogy, we have to consider many things—the objectives of education, the curriculum, how assessment strategies work, the kind of technology infrastructure involved, and how leadership and policy facilitate attaining education goals."
Chris Dede, Harvard University
_____
_____
_____
_____

Daily Planner

Date: _____

To do

Morning _____

_____

_____

_____

_____

_____

_____

_____

Afternoon _____

_____

_____

_____

_____

_____

_____

Evening _____

_____

_____

_____

_____

_____

_____

Goals

_____

_____

_____

_____

Appointments

_____

_____

Call / Email

_____

_____

Meal Planner

_____

_____

Water Intake

○ ○ ○ ○
○ ○ ○ ○

Steps _____

Notes

The illiterate of the future will not be the person who cannot read. It will be the person who does not know how to learn. Alvin Toffler

_____

_____

_____

_____

_____

_____

_____

_____

Daily Planner

Date: _____

To do

Morning _____

_____

_____

_____

_____

_____

_____

_____

Afternoon _____

_____

_____

_____

_____

_____

_____

Evening _____

_____

_____

_____

_____

_____

_____

Goals

_____

_____

_____

_____

_____

Appointments

_____

_____

_____

Call / Email

_____

_____

Meal Planner

_____

_____

_____

Water Intake

◯ ◯ ◯ ◯
◯ ◯ ◯ ◯

Steps _____

Notes

"Every child deserves a teacher who believes in them.
Be that one!"
Phil Schlechty, Founder, Schlechty Center

_____

_____

_____

_____

_____

_____

_____

Daily Planner

Date: _____

To do

Morning _____

_____

_____

_____

_____

_____

_____

_____

Afternoon _____

_____

_____

_____

_____

_____

_____

Evening _____

_____

_____

_____

_____

_____

_____

Goals

_____

_____

_____

_____

_____

Appointments

_____

_____

_____

Call / Email

_____

_____

_____

Meal Planner

_____

_____

Water Intake

○ ○ ○
○ ○ ○

Steps _____

Notes

"School is not about transmitting information. Kids can get any information they want. The trick is to motivate them to want to get the right information and then give them a choice about how to get that information."
Phil Schlechty, Founder, Schlechty Center

_____

_____

_____

_____

_____

Daily Planner

Date: _____

To do

Morning _____

_____

_____

_____

_____

_____

_____

_____

Afternoon _____

_____

_____

_____

_____

_____

_____

_____

Evening _____

_____

_____

_____

_____

_____

_____

_____

Goals

_____

_____

_____

_____

_____

Appointments

_____

_____

Call / Email

_____

_____

Meal Planner

_____

_____

Water Intake

○ ○ ○ ○
○ ○ ○ ○

Steps _____

Notes

"There is no single best way to teach because there is no single best way to learn."
Chris Dede, Harvard University

_____

_____

_____

_____

_____

_____

_____

workout log

Week

Date : _____ Time : _____ Week : _____

Workout Day : ① ② ③ ④ ⑤ ⑥ ⑦

Exercise	Reps	Set -1	Set -2	Set -3	Set -4	Set -5

Date : _____ Time : _____ Week : _____

Workout Day : ① ② ③ ④ ⑤ ⑥ ⑦

Exercise	Reps	Set -1	Set -2	Set -3	Set -4	Set -5

Weight

Body Fat

Chest

Right Arm

Left Arm

Waist

Hips

Right Leg

Left Leg

To Do List This Week

Day _____

Date & Month _____

No.	To Do	Yes/No	
___	_____	☐	☐
___	_____	☐	☐
___	_____	☐	☐
___	_____	☐	☐
___	_____	☐	☐
___	_____	☐	☐
___	_____	☐	☐
___	_____	☐	☐
___	_____	☐	☐
___	_____	☐	☐
___	_____	☐	☐
___	_____	☐	☐
___	_____	☐	☐
___	_____	☐	☐
___	_____	☐	☐
___	_____	☐	☐
___	_____	☐	☐
___	_____	☐	☐
___	_____	☐	☐

Notes _____

_____

_____

_____

Daily Planner

Date: _____

To do

Morning _____
_____
_____
_____
_____
_____
_____

Afternoon _____
_____
_____
_____
_____
_____
_____

Evening _____
_____
_____
_____
_____
_____
_____

Goals
_____
_____
_____
_____

Appointments
_____
_____

Call / Email
_____
_____

Meal Planner
_____
_____

Water Intake
◯ ◯ ◯
◯ ◯ ◯

Steps _____

Notes

The biggest atrocity of all is to indoctrinate our children into a system that does not value their creative expression, nor encourage their unique abilities. Benjamin Greene

_____
_____
_____
_____
_____

Daily Planner

Date: _____

To do

Morning _____

_____
_____
_____
_____
_____
_____
_____

Afternoon _____

_____
_____
_____
_____
_____
_____

Evening _____

_____
_____
_____
_____
_____
_____

Goals

_____
_____
_____
_____
_____

Appointments

_____
_____

Call / Email

_____
_____

Meal Planner

_____
_____

Water Intake

○ ○ ○ ○
○ ○ ○ ○

Steps _____

Notes

The aim of education should be to teach us how to think, rather than what to think. To improve our minds, so as to enable us to think for ourselves, rather than to load the memory with thoughts of other men. Bill Beattie

_____
_____
_____
_____
_____

Daily Planner

Date: _____

To do

Morning _____

_____

_____

_____

_____

_____

_____

_____

Afternoon _____

_____

_____

_____

_____

_____

_____

Evening _____

_____

_____

_____

_____

_____

Goals

_____

_____

_____

_____

Appointments

_____

_____

Call / Email

_____

_____

Meal Planner

_____

_____

Water Intake

◯ ◯ ◯ ◯
◯ ◯ ◯ ◯

Steps _____

Notes

I never teach my pupils. I only attempt to provide the conditions in which they can learn. Albert Einstein

_____

_____

_____

_____

_____

Daily Planner

Date: _____

To do

Morning _____

_____

_____

_____

_____

_____

_____

_____

Afternoon _____

_____

_____

_____

_____

_____

_____

Evening _____

_____

_____

_____

_____

_____

_____

Goals

_____

_____

_____

_____

_____

Appointments

_____

_____

Call / Email

_____

_____

Meal Planner

_____

_____

Water Intake

○ ○ ○ ○
○ ○ ○ ○

Steps _____

Notes

Lifelong learning = ongoing, voluntary, & self-motivated pursuit of knowledge. – Craig Kemp

_____

_____

_____

_____

_____

_____

_____

Daily Planner

Date: _____

To do

Morning _____

_____

_____

_____

_____

_____

_____

_____

Afternoon _____

_____

_____

_____

_____

_____

_____

Evening _____

_____

_____

_____

_____

_____

_____

Goals

_____

_____

_____

_____

_____

Appointments

_____

_____

_____

Call / Email

_____

_____

_____

Meal Planner

_____

_____

Water Intake

◯ ◯ ◯
◯ ◯ ◯

Steps _____

Notes

Yes, kids love technology, but they also love Legos, scented markers, handstands, books and mud puddles. It's all about balance.

_____

_____

_____

_____

_____

_____

_____

_____

Daily Planner

Date: _____

To do

Morning _____

_____
_____
_____
_____
_____
_____
_____

Afternoon _____

_____
_____
_____
_____
_____
_____

Evening _____

_____
_____
_____
_____
_____
_____

Goals

_____
_____
_____
_____
_____

Appointments

_____
_____
_____

Call / Email

_____
_____
_____

Meal Planner

_____
_____

Water Intake

○ ○ ○ ○
○ ○ ○ ○

Steps _____

Notes

Teaching should be such that what is offered is perceived as a valuable gift and not as a hard duty.
Albert Einstein

_____
_____
_____
_____
_____
_____
_____

Daily Planner

Date: _____

To do

Morning _____

_____

_____

_____

_____

_____

_____

_____

Afternoon _____

_____

_____

_____

_____

_____

_____

_____

Evening _____

_____

_____

_____

_____

_____

_____

Goals

_____

_____

_____

_____

_____

Appointments

_____

_____

Call / Email

_____

_____

Meal Planner

_____

_____

Water Intake

◯ ◯ ◯
◯ ◯ ◯

Steps _____

Notes

The one real object of education is to have a man in the condition of continually asking questions. Bishop Mandell Creighton

_____

_____

_____

_____

_____

_____

workout log

Week

Date : _____ Time : _____ Week : _____

Workout Day : ① ② ③ ④ ⑤ ⑥ ⑦

Exercise	Reps	Set -1	Set -2	Set -3	Set -4	Set -5

Date : _____ Time : _____ Week : _____

Workout Day : ① ② ③ ④ ⑤ ⑥ ⑦

Exercise	Reps	Set -1	Set -2	Set -3	Set -4	Set -5

Weight

Body Fat

Chest

Right Arm

Left Arm

Waist

Hips

Right Leg

Left Leg

To Do List This Week

Day _____

Date & Month _____

No.	To Do	Yes/No
		☐ ☐
		☐ ☐
		☐ ☐
		☐ ☐
		☐ ☐
		☐ ☐
		☐ ☐
		☐ ☐
		☐ ☐
		☐ ☐
		☐ ☐
		☐ ☐
		☐ ☐
		☐ ☐
		☐ ☐
		☐ ☐
		☐ ☐
		☐ ☐
		☐ ☐
		☐ ☐

Notes _____

_____

_____

_____

Date: _____

To do

Morning _____

_____

_____

_____

_____

_____

_____

_____

Afternoon _____

_____

_____

_____

_____

_____

_____

Evening _____

_____

_____

_____

_____

_____

_____

Goals

_____

_____

_____

_____

_____

Appointments

_____

_____

_____

Call / Email

_____

_____

Meal Planner

_____

_____

_____

Water Intake

○ ○ ○ ○
○ ○ ○ ○

Steps _____

Notes

If I ran a school, I'd give the average grade to the ones who gave me all the right answers, for being good parrots. I'd give the top grades to those who made a lot of mistakes and told me about them, and then told me what they learned from them.
Buckminster Fuller

_____

_____

_____

_____

_____

Daily Planner

Date: _____

To do

Morning _____

_____
_____
_____
_____
_____
_____
_____

Afternoon _____

_____
_____
_____
_____
_____
_____

Evening _____

_____
_____
_____
_____
_____
_____

Goals

_____
_____
_____
_____
_____

Appointments

_____
_____

Call / Email

_____
_____

Meal Planner

_____
_____

Water Intake

○ ○ ○
○ ○ ○

Steps _____

Notes

It is the supreme art of the teacher to awaken joy in creative expression and knowledge. Albert Einstein

_____
_____
_____
_____
_____

Daily Planner

Date: _____

To do

Morning _____

_____

_____

_____

_____

_____

_____

_____

Afternoon _____

_____

_____

_____

_____

_____

_____

Evening _____

_____

_____

_____

_____

_____

_____

Goals

_____

_____

_____

_____

_____

Appointments

_____

_____

Call / Email

_____

_____

Meal Planner

_____

_____

Water Intake

◯ ◯ ◯
◯ ◯ ◯

Steps _____

Notes

Teachers should guide without dictating, and participate without dominating. C. B. Neblette

_____

_____

_____

_____

_____

_____

_____

Daily Planner

Date: _____

To do

Morning _____

_____

_____

_____

_____

_____

_____

_____

_____

_____

Afternoon _____

_____

_____

_____

_____

_____

_____

_____

_____

_____

Evening _____

_____

_____

_____

_____

_____

_____

_____

Goals

_____

_____

_____

_____

_____

_____

Appointments

_____

_____

_____

Call / Email

_____

_____

_____

Meal Planner

_____

_____

Water Intake

○ ○ ○
○ ○ ○

Steps _____

Notes

One looks back with appreciation to the brilliant teachers, but with gratitude to those who touched our human feelings. The curriculum is so much necessary raw material, but warmth is a vital element for the growing plant and for the soul of the child. Carl Jung

_____

_____

_____

_____

Daily Planner

Date: _____

To do

Morning _____

_____

_____

_____

_____

_____

_____

_____

Afternoon _____

_____

_____

_____

_____

_____

_____

Evening _____

_____

_____

_____

_____

_____

_____

Goals

_____

_____

_____

_____

Appointments

_____

_____

Call / Email

_____

_____

Meal Planner

_____

_____

Water Intake

○ ○ ○ ○
○ ○ ○ ○

Steps _____

Notes

If we value independence, if we are disturbed by the growing conformity of knowledge, then we may wish to set up conditions of learning which make for uniqueness. Carl Rogers

_____

_____

_____

_____

_____

_____

Daily Planner

Date: _____

To do

Morning _____
_____
_____
_____
_____
_____
_____
_____

Afternoon _____
_____
_____
_____
_____
_____
_____

Evening _____
_____
_____
_____
_____
_____
_____
_____

Goals
_____
_____
_____
_____

Appointments
_____
_____

Call / Email
_____
_____

Meal Planner
_____
_____

Water Intake
◯ ◯ ◯ ◯
◯ ◯ ◯ ◯

Steps _____

Notes

Self-education is the only possible education; the rest is mere veneer laid on the surface of a child's nature.
Charlotte Mason
_____
_____
_____
_____
_____

Daily Planner

Date: _____

To do

Morning _____
_____
_____
_____
_____
_____
_____
_____

Afternoon _____
_____
_____
_____
_____
_____
_____

Evening _____
_____
_____
_____
_____
_____
_____

Goals
_____
_____
_____
_____

Appointments
_____
_____

Call / Email
_____
_____

Meal Planner
_____
_____

Water Intake
◯ ◯ ◯ ◯
◯ ◯ ◯ ◯

Steps _____

Notes
Teaching is far from perfect. It's messy, and it's in that mess that you will craft your teaching and really enjoy the journey. Lisa Dabbs, Educator
_____
_____
_____
_____
_____
_____

workout log

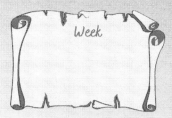

Week

Date : _____ Time : _____ Week : _____

Workout Day : ① ② ③ ④ ⑤ ⑥ ⑦

Exercise	Reps	Set -1	Set -2	Set -3	Set -4	Set -5

Weight

Body Fat

Chest

Right Arm

Left Arm

Waist

Hips

Right Leg

Left Leg

Date : _____ Time : _____ Week : _____

Workout Day : ① ② ③ ④ ⑤ ⑥ ⑦

Exercise	Reps	Set -1	Set -2	Set -3	Set -4	Set -5

To Do List This Week

Day _____

Date & Month _____

No.	To Do	Yes/No	
___	_____	☐	☐
___	_____	☐	☐
___	_____	☐	☐
___	_____	☐	☐
___	_____	☐	☐
___	_____	☐	☐
___	_____	☐	☐
___	_____	☐	☐
___	_____	☐	☐
___	_____	☐	☐
___	_____	☐	☐
___	_____	☐	☐
___	_____	☐	☐
___	_____	☐	☐
___	_____	☐	☐
___	_____	☐	☐
___	_____	☐	☐
___	_____	☐	☐
___	_____	☐	☐

Notes _____

_____

_____

_____

Daily Planner

Date: _____

To do

Morning _____

_____

_____

_____

_____

_____

_____

Afternoon _____

_____

_____

_____

_____

_____

_____

Evening _____

_____

_____

_____

_____

_____

_____

Goals

_____

_____

_____

_____

_____

_____

Appointments

_____

_____

Call / Email

_____

_____

Meal Planner

_____

_____

Water Intake

◯ ◯ ◯ ◯
◯ ◯ ◯ ◯

Steps _____

Notes

Of all the joyous motives of school life, the love of knowledge is the only abiding one; the only one which determines the scale, so to speak, upon which the person will hereafter live.

Charlotte Mason

_____

_____

_____

_____

_____

Date: _____

To do

Morning _____

_____
_____
_____
_____
_____
_____
_____
_____

Afternoon _____

_____
_____
_____
_____
_____
_____
_____

Evening _____

_____
_____
_____
_____
_____
_____
_____

Goals

_____
_____
_____
_____
_____
_____

Appointments

_____
_____
_____

Call / Email

_____
_____

Meal Planner

_____
_____

Water Intake

○ ○ ○
○ ○ ○

Steps _____

Notes

Technology can become the "wings" that will allow the educational world to fly farther and faster than ever before—if we will allow it. Jenny Arledge

_____
_____
_____
_____
_____
_____

Daily Planner

Date: _____

To do

Morning _____

_____

_____

_____

_____

_____

_____

Afternoon _____

_____

_____

_____

_____

_____

Evening _____

_____

_____

_____

_____

_____

Goals

_____

_____

_____

_____

_____

Appointments

_____

_____

Call / Email

_____

_____

Meal Planner

_____

_____

Water Intake

○ ○ ○ ○
○ ○ ○ ○

Steps _____

Notes

If you are planning for a year, sow rice; if you are planning for a decade, plant trees; if you are planning for a lifetime, educate people.
Chinese proverb

_____

_____

_____

_____

_____

_____

Date: _____

To do

Morning _____

_____

_____

_____

_____

_____

_____

_____

Afternoon _____

_____

_____

_____

_____

_____

_____

Evening _____

_____

_____

_____

_____

_____

Goals

_____

_____

_____

_____

_____

Appointments

_____

_____

Call / Email

_____

_____

Meal Planner

_____

_____

Water Intake

○ ○ ○ ○
○ ○ ○ ○

Steps _____

Notes

At the end of the day, it's not about what you have or even what you've accomplished. It's about what you've done with those accomplishments. It's about who you've lifted up, who you've made better. It's about what you've given back."
Denzel Washington

_____

_____

_____

_____

_____

_____

Daily Planner

Date: _____

To do

Morning _____
_____
_____
_____
_____
_____
_____

Afternoon _____
_____
_____
_____
_____
_____
_____

Evening _____
_____
_____
_____
_____
_____
_____

Goals

_____
_____
_____
_____
_____

Appointments

_____
_____

Call / Email

_____
_____

Meal Planner

_____
_____

Water Intake

◯ ◯ ◯
◯ ◯ ◯

Steps _____

Notes

"We will all, at some point, encounter hurdles to gaining access and entry, moving up and conquering self-doubt; but on the other side is the capacity to own opportunity and tell our own story." —Stacey Abrams

_____
_____
_____
_____
_____
_____

Daily Planner

Date: _____

To do

Morning _____

_____

_____

_____

_____

_____

_____

_____

Afternoon _____

_____

_____

_____

_____

_____

_____

Evening _____

_____

_____

_____

_____

_____

_____

Goals

_____

_____

_____

_____

_____

Appointments

_____

_____

_____

Call / Email

_____

_____

_____

Meal Planner

_____

_____

Water Intake

◯ ◯ ◯ ◯
◯ ◯ ◯ ◯

Steps _____

Notes

"We're bosses, and that's what I consider feminism: female hustlers." —Cardi B

_____

_____

_____

_____

_____

_____

_____

_____

Daily Planner

Date: _____

To do

Morning _____
_____
_____
_____
_____
_____
_____
_____

Afternoon _____
_____
_____
_____
_____
_____
_____

Evening _____
_____
_____
_____
_____
_____
_____
_____

Goals
_____
_____
_____
_____
_____

Appointments
_____
_____

Call / Email
_____
_____

Meal Planner
_____
_____

Water Intake
◯ ◯ ◯ ◯
◯ ◯ ◯ ◯

Steps _____

Notes

"Success? I don't know what that word means. I'm happy. But success, that goes back to what in somebody's eyes success means. For me, success is inner peace. That's a good day for me."
Denzel Washington

_____
_____
_____
_____
_____
_____

MY MEETING NOTES

MEETING NAME & DATE -

ATTENDEES -

NEXT STEPS / DEADLINES -

MEETING NOTES -

"Somebody once said we never know what is enough until we know what's more than enough." —Billie Holiday

MY MEETING NOTES

MEETING NAME & DATE -

ATTENDEES -

NEXT STEPS / DEADLINES -

MEETING NOTES -

_____

_____

_____

_____

_____

_____

_____

_____

_____

_____

_____

_____

_____

_____

_____

_____

_____

_____

_____

"My humanity is bound up in yours, for we can only be human together." —Desmond Tutu

MY MEETING NOTES

MEETING NAME & DATE -

ATTENDEES -

NEXT STEPS / DEADLINES -

MEETING NOTES -

_____

_____

_____

_____

_____

_____

_____

_____

_____

_____

_____

_____

_____

_____

_____

_____

_____

_____

_____

_____

"If you prioritize yourself, you are going to save yourself." —Gabrielle Union

MY MEETING NOTES

MEETING NAME & DATE -

ATTENDEES -

NEXT STEPS / DEADLINES -

MEETING NOTES -

_____
_____
_____
_____
_____
_____
_____
_____
_____
_____
_____
_____
_____
_____
_____
_____
_____
_____
_____

"If you have a chance to accomplish something that will make things better for people coming behind you, and you don't do that, you are wasting your time on this earth."
Roberto Clemente

MY MEETING NOTES

MEETING NAME & DATE -

ATTENDEES -

NEXT STEPS / DEADLINES -

MEETING NOTES -

_____
_____
_____
_____
_____
_____
_____
_____
_____
_____
_____
_____
_____
_____
_____
_____
_____
_____
_____
_____

"I have standards I don't plan on lowering for anybody, including myself." —Zendaya

MY MEETING NOTES

MEETING NAME & DATE -

ATTENDEES -

NEXT STEPS / DEADLINES -

MEETING NOTES -

"Sometimes, I feel discriminated against, but it does not make me angry. It merely astonishes me. How can any deny themselves the pleasure of my company? It's beyond me."
Zora Neale Hurston

MY MEETING NOTES

MEETING NAME & DATE -

ATTENDEES -

NEXT STEPS / DEADLINES -

MEETING NOTES -

"Women make up more than half of the world's population and potential. So it is neither just nor practical for their voices, for our voices, to go unheard at the highest levels of decision-making." —Meghan Markle

MY MEETING NOTES

MEETING NAME & DATE -

ATTENDEES -

NEXT STEPS / DEADLINES -

MEETING NOTES -

_____

_____

_____

_____

_____

_____

_____

_____

_____

_____

_____

_____

_____

_____

_____

_____

_____

_____

_____

"Embrace what makes you unique, even if it makes others uncomfortable. I didn't have to become perfect because I've learned throughout my journey that perfection is the enemy of greatness." —Janelle Monae

MY MEETING NOTES

MEETING NAME & DATE -

ATTENDEES -

NEXT STEPS / DEADLINES -

MEETING NOTES -

_____

_____

_____

_____

_____

_____

_____

_____

_____

_____

_____

_____

_____

_____

_____

_____

_____

_____

_____

_____

"You are not and yet you are: your thoughts, your deeds, above all your dreams still live."
W.E.B. Du Bois

MY MEETING NOTES

MEETING NAME & DATE -

ATTENDEES -

NEXT STEPS / DEADLINES -

MEETING NOTES -

"Your story is what you have, what you will always have. It is something to own."
Michelle Obama

MY MEETING NOTES

MEETING NAME & DATE -

ATTENDEES -

NEXT STEPS / DEADLINES -

MEETING NOTES -

"I feel safe in the midst of my enemies, for the truth is all powerful and will prevail."
Sojourner Truth

MY MEETING NOTES

MEETING NAME & DATE -

ATTENDEES -

NEXT STEPS / DEADLINES -

MEETING NOTES -

"It's important for young people to know that they are made the way they are made and they're beautiful and that's how they're supposed to be." —Raven Symone

MONTHLY REVIEW

THIS MONTH I ACHIEVED

_____
_____
_____
_____
_____
_____
_____
_____
_____

WHAT WORKED

_____
_____
_____
_____

WHAT DIDN'T WORK

_____
_____
_____
_____

DO MORE OF

_____
_____
_____
_____
_____

DO LESS OF

_____
_____
_____
_____
_____

MONTHLY REVIEW

MONTH OF

THIS MONTH I ACHIEVED

_____

_____

_____

_____

_____

_____

_____

_____

WHAT WORKED

_____

_____

_____

_____

WHAT DIDN'T WORK

_____

_____

_____

_____

DO MORE OF

DO LESS OF

MARCH

MON
LEGS

Stretching and warm-up
25 Squats
25 Sumo Squats
Repeat above March in place for 20 sec
Stretch muscles
Relax

TUES
ABS

Stretching and warm-up
20 Standing Oblique Twists
30-second Floor Plank
Repeat above
March in place for 20 seconds
Stretch muscles
Relax

WED
ARMS

Stretching and warm-up
25 Push-ups
20 Wall Tricep Pushes
Repeat above
March in place for 20
seconds
Stretch muscles
Relax

THURS
CARDIO

Stretching and warm-up
50 Jumping Jacks
30-second Sprint in place
Repeat above
March in place for 20
seconds
Stretch muscles
Relax

FRI
COMBO

Stretching and warm-up
10 Squats & 10 Sumo
Squats
10 Standing Oblique Twists
March in place for 20
seconds
20 Push-ups
25 Jumping Jacks
March in place for 20
seconds
Stretch muscles
Relax

SAT
YOUR PICK

Choose from Day 1-4
to work on your chosen area:
Legs
Abs
Arms or
Cardio

SUN
REST

Take a break!
You deserve it.

workout log

Week

Date: _____ Time: _____ Week: _____

Workout Day: ① ② ③ ④ ⑤ ⑥ ⑦

Exercise	Reps	Set -1	Set -2	Set -3	Set -4	Set -5

Date: _____ Time: _____ Week: _____

Workout Day: ① ② ③ ④ ⑤ ⑥ ⑦

Exercise	Reps	Set -1	Set -2	Set -3	Set -4	Set -5

Weight

Body Fat

Chest

Right Arm

Left Arm

Waist

Hips

Right Leg

Left Leg

THIS MONTH'S LIST

Month: March Year: _____

Potential Items to Plan/Schedule:
District Board Mtg
District Principal Mtg
Campus Admin Mtg
Vertical Team Mtg
Parent Conferences
LPACs/ELLs/ARDs
Progress Reports/Report Cards
Master Schedule Review
Team Leader/Dept. Chair Mtg
Professional Learning Community (PLC) Mtg
Athletic Event Admin Coverage Schedule
Teachers I need to meet with (observe/walkthrough)

Potential Assessments
Campus Level Assessments-State Aligned Objectives

Additions
Shared Decision Making Council (SDMC)
Picture Day Planning
State Testing Planning & Roster Development

_____
_____
_____
_____
_____
_____
_____
_____
_____

MONTHLY PLANNER
MONTH: _____

MONDAY	TUESDAY	WEDNESDAY	THURSDAY	FRIDAY	SATURDAY	SUNDAY

PRIORITY

Daily Planner

Date: _____

To do

Morning _____

_____

_____

_____

_____

_____

_____

_____

Afternoon _____

_____

_____

_____

_____

_____

_____

Evening _____

_____

_____

_____

_____

_____

_____

Goals

_____

_____

_____

_____

_____

Appointments

_____

_____

_____

Call / Email

_____

_____

_____

Meal Planner

_____

_____

Water Intake

◯ ◯ ◯ ◯
◯ ◯ ◯ ◯

Steps _____

Notes

You can teach a student a lesson for a day; but if you can teach him to learn by creating curiosity, he will continue the learning process as long as he lives. Clay P. Bedford

_____

_____

_____

_____

_____

Daily Planner

Date: _____

To do

Morning _____

_____

_____

_____

_____

_____

_____

Afternoon _____

_____

_____

_____

_____

_____

_____

Evening _____

_____

_____

_____

_____

_____

_____

_____

Goals

_____

_____

_____

_____

_____

Appointments

_____

_____

Call / Email

_____

_____

Meal Planner

_____

_____

Water Intake

◯ ◯ ◯ ◯
◯ ◯ ◯ ◯

Steps _____

Notes

Education is soul crafting. Cornel West

_____

_____

_____

_____

_____

_____

_____

Daily Planner

Date: _____

To do

Morning _____

_____

_____

_____

_____

_____

_____

_____

Afternoon _____

_____

_____

_____

_____

_____

_____

Evening _____

_____

_____

_____

_____

_____

Goals

_____

_____

_____

_____

_____

Appointments

_____

_____

Call / Email

_____

_____

Meal Planner

_____

_____

Water Intake

◯ ◯ ◯ ◯
◯ ◯ ◯ ◯

Steps _____

Notes

Children want the same things we want. To laugh, to be challenged, to be entertained, and delighted.
Dr. Seuss

_____

_____

_____

_____

_____

_____

_____

Daily Planner

Date: _____

To do

Morning _____

_____

_____

_____

_____

_____

_____

_____

Afternoon _____

_____

_____

_____

_____

_____

_____

Evening _____

_____

_____

_____

_____

_____

_____

Goals

_____

_____

_____

_____

_____

Appointments

_____

_____

Call / Email

_____

_____

Meal Planner

_____

_____

Water Intake

◯ ◯ ◯
◯ ◯ ◯

Steps _____

Notes

For the sole true end of education is simply this: to teach men how to learn for themselves; and whatever instruction fails to do this is effort spent in vain. Dorothy L. Sayers

_____

_____

_____

_____

_____

_____

Daily Planner

Date: _____

To do

Morning _____

_____

_____

_____

_____

_____

_____

_____

Afternoon _____

_____

_____

_____

_____

_____

_____

_____

Evening _____

_____

_____

_____

_____

_____

_____

Goals

_____

_____

_____

_____

_____

Appointments

_____

_____

_____

Call / Email

_____

_____

Meal Planner

_____

_____

_____

Water Intake

◯ ◯ ◯
◯ ◯ ◯

Steps _____

Notes

I like a teacher who gives you something to take home to think about besides homework.
Edith Ann [Lily Tomlin]

_____

_____

_____

_____

_____

_____

Daily Planner

Date: _____

To do

Morning _____

_____

_____

_____

_____

_____

_____

Afternoon _____

_____

_____

_____

_____

_____

Evening _____

_____

_____

_____

_____

_____

Goals

_____

_____

_____

_____

Appointments

_____

_____

Call / Email

_____

_____

Meal Planner

_____

_____

Water Intake

○ ○ ○ ○
○ ○ ○ ○

Steps _____

Notes

In a time of drastic change, it is the learners who inherit the future. The learned usually find themselves equipped to live in a world that no longer exists. Eric Hoffer

_____

_____

_____

_____

_____

_____

Daily Planner

Date: _____

To do

Morning _____

_____

_____

_____

_____

_____

_____

_____

Afternoon _____

_____

_____

_____

_____

_____

_____

Evening _____

_____

_____

_____

_____

_____

_____

Goals

_____

_____

_____

_____

_____

Appointments

_____

_____

Call / Email

_____

_____

Meal Planner

_____

_____

Water Intake

◯ ◯ ◯ ◯
◯ ◯ ◯ ◯

Steps _____

Notes

My schooling not only failed to teach me what it professed to be teaching but prevented me from being educated to an extent which infuriates me when I think of all I might have learned at home by myself. George Bernard Shaw

_____

_____

_____

_____

_____

workout log

Week

Date : _____ Time : _____ Week : _____

| Workout Day : | ① | ② | ③ | ④ | ⑤ | ⑥ | ⑦ |

Exercise	Reps	Set -1	Set -2	Set -3	Set -4	Set -5

Date : _____ Time : _____ Week : _____

| Workout Day : | ① | ② | ③ | ④ | ⑤ | ⑥ | ⑦ |

Exercise	Reps	Set -1	Set -2	Set -3	Set -4	Set -5

Weight

Body Fat

Chest

Right Arm

Left Arm

Waist

Hips

Right Leg

Left Leg

To Do List This Week

Day _____

Date & Month _____

No.	To Do	Yes/No	
___	_____	☐	☐
___	_____	☐	☐
___	_____	☐	☐
___	_____	☐	☐
___	_____	☐	☐
___	_____	☐	☐
___	_____	☐	☐
___	_____	☐	☐
___	_____	☐	☐
___	_____	☐	☐
___	_____	☐	☐
___	_____	☐	☐
___	_____	☐	☐
___	_____	☐	☐
___	_____	☐	☐
___	_____	☐	☐
___	_____	☐	☐
___	_____	☐	☐
___	_____	☐	☐
___	_____	☐	☐

Notes _____

_____

_____

_____

Daily Planner

Date: _____

To do

Morning _____
_____
_____
_____
_____
_____
_____

Afternoon _____
_____
_____
_____
_____
_____
_____

Evening _____
_____
_____
_____
_____
_____
_____

Goals
_____
_____
_____
_____

Appointments
_____
_____

Call / Email
_____
_____

Meal Planner
_____
_____

Water Intake
○ ○ ○ ○
○ ○ ○ ○

Steps _____

Notes
Every student can learn. Just not on the same day or in the same way. George Evans
_____
_____
_____
_____
_____
_____

Daily Planner

Date: _____

To do

Morning _____

_____

_____

_____

_____

_____

_____

Afternoon _____

_____

_____

_____

_____

_____

_____

Evening _____

_____

_____

_____

_____

_____

_____

Goals

_____

_____

_____

_____

Appointments

_____

_____

Call / Email

_____

_____

Meal Planner

_____

_____

Water Intake

○ ○ ○
○ ○ ○ ○

Steps _____

Notes

A child educated only at school is an uneducated child. George Santayana

_____

_____

_____

_____

_____

_____

_____

Daily Planner

Date: _____

To do

Morning _____

_____

_____

_____

_____

_____

_____

_____

Afternoon _____

_____

_____

_____

_____

_____

_____

Evening _____

_____

_____

_____

_____

_____

_____

Goals

_____

_____

_____

_____

_____

Appointments

_____

_____

_____

Call / Email

_____

_____

_____

Meal Planner

_____

_____

Water Intake

○ ○ ○ ○
○ ○ ○ ○

Steps _____

Notes

What we want is to see the child in pursuit of knowledge, and not knowledge in pursuit of the child. George Bernard Shaw

_____

_____

_____

_____

_____

_____

_____

_____

Daily Planner

Date: _____

To do

Morning _____
_____
_____
_____
_____
_____
_____
_____

Afternoon _____
_____
_____
_____
_____
_____
_____
_____

Evening _____
_____
_____
_____
_____
_____
_____
_____

Goals

_____
_____
_____
_____
_____

Appointments

_____
_____

Call / Email

_____
_____

Meal Planner

_____
_____

Water Intake

○ ○ ○
○ ○ ○

Steps _____

Notes

Children want to learn to the degree that they are unable to distinguish learning from fun. They keep this attitude until we adults convince them that learning is not fun.
Glenn Doman

_____
_____
_____
_____
_____

Date: _____

To do

Goals

Morning _____

_____

_____

_____

_____

_____

_____

_____

Afternoon _____

_____

_____

_____

_____

_____

_____

_____

Evening _____

_____

_____

_____

_____

_____

_____

_____

Goals

_____

_____

_____

_____

_____

Appointments

_____

_____

_____

Call / Email

_____

_____

_____

Meal Planner

_____

_____

_____

Water Intake

◯ ◯ ◯ ◯
◯ ◯ ◯ ◯

Steps _____

Notes

In an effective classroom students should not only know what they are doing, they should also know why and how. Harry K. Wong

_____

_____

_____

_____

_____

_____

_____

Daily Planner

Date: _____

To do

Morning _____

_____

_____

_____

_____

_____

_____

_____

Afternoon _____

_____

_____

_____

_____

_____

_____

_____

Evening _____

_____

_____

_____

_____

_____

_____

_____

Goals

_____

_____

_____

_____

_____

Appointments

_____

_____

_____

Call / Email

_____

_____

Meal Planner

_____

_____

Water Intake

○ ○ ○ ○
○ ○ ○ ○

Steps _____

Notes

We should seek to be fellow students with the pupil, and should learn of, as well as with him, if we would be most helpful to him. Henry David Thoreau

_____

_____

_____

_____

_____

Daily Planner

Date: _____

To do

Morning _____

_____

_____

_____

_____

_____

_____

_____

Afternoon _____

_____

_____

_____

_____

_____

_____

Evening _____

_____

_____

_____

_____

_____

_____

Goals

_____

_____

_____

_____

_____

Appointments

_____

_____

_____

Call / Email

_____

_____

_____

Meal Planner

_____

_____

Water Intake

◯ ◯ ◯ ◯
◯ ◯ ◯ ◯

Steps _____

Notes

A teacher who is attempting to teach without inspiring the pupil with a desire to learn is hammering on cold iron. Horace Mann

_____

_____

_____

_____

_____

_____

_____

workout log

Week

Date: _____ Time: _____ Week: _____

Workout Day: ① ② ③ ④ ⑤ ⑥ ⑦

Exercise	Reps	Set -1	Set -2	Set -3	Set -4	Set -5

Date: _____ Time: _____ Week: _____

Workout Day: ① ② ③ ④ ⑤ ⑥ ⑦

Exercise	Reps	Set -1	Set -2	Set -3	Set -4	Set -5

Weight

Body Fat

Chest

Right Arm

Left Arm

Waist

Hips

Right Leg

Left Leg

To Do List This Week

Day _____

Date & Month _____

No.	To Do	Yes/No	
_____	_____	☐	☐
_____	_____	☐	☐
_____	_____	☐	☐
_____	_____	☐	☐
_____	_____	☐	☐
_____	_____	☐	☐
_____	_____	☐	☐
_____	_____	☐	☐
_____	_____	☐	☐
_____	_____	☐	☐
_____	_____	☐	☐
_____	_____	☐	☐
_____	_____	☐	☐
_____	_____	☐	☐
_____	_____	☐	☐
_____	_____	☐	☐
_____	_____	☐	☐
_____	_____	☐	☐
_____	_____	☐	☐
_____	_____	☐	☐

Notes _____

_____

_____

_____

Daily Planner

Date: _____

To do

Morning _____
_____
_____
_____
_____
_____
_____
_____

Afternoon _____
_____
_____
_____
_____
_____
_____
_____
_____

Evening _____
_____
_____
_____
_____
_____
_____
_____

Goals

_____
_____
_____
_____
_____

Appointments

_____
_____
_____

Call / Email

_____
_____
_____

Meal Planner

_____
_____
_____

Water Intake

◯ ◯ ◯ ◯
◯ ◯ ◯ ◯

Steps _____

Notes

If a child can't learn the way we teach, maybe we should teach the way they learn. Ignacio Estrada

_____
_____
_____
_____
_____
_____

Date: _____

To do

Morning _____

_____

_____

_____

_____

_____

_____

Afternoon _____

_____

_____

_____

_____

_____

Evening _____

_____

_____

_____

_____

_____

_____

Goals

_____

_____

_____

_____

Appointments

_____

_____

Call / Email

_____

_____

Meal Planner

_____

_____

Water Intake

○ ○ ○ ○
○ ○ ○ ○

Steps _____

Notes

Teaching is a strategic act of engagement.
James Bellanca

_____

_____

_____

_____

_____

_____

_____

Daily Planner

Date: _____

To do

Morning _____
_____
_____
_____
_____
_____
_____
_____
_____

Afternoon _____
_____
_____
_____
_____
_____
_____
_____

Evening _____
_____
_____
_____
_____
_____
_____

Goals
_____
_____
_____
_____
_____

Appointments
_____
_____

Call / Email
_____
_____

Meal Planner
_____
_____

Water Intake
○ ○ ○ ○
○ ○ ○ ○

Steps _____

Notes

The principle goal of education is to create men and women who are capable of doing new things, not simply repeating what other generations have done. Jean Piaget
_____
_____
_____
_____
_____
_____
_____

Daily Planner

Date: _____

To do

Morning _____

_____

_____

_____

_____

_____

_____

_____

Afternoon _____

_____

_____

_____

_____

_____

_____

_____

Evening _____

_____

_____

_____

_____

_____

_____

_____

Goals

_____

_____

_____

_____

_____

Appointments

_____

_____

_____

Call / Email

_____

_____

_____

Meal Planner

_____

_____

_____

Water Intake

◯ ◯ ◯ ◯
◯ ◯ ◯ ◯

Steps _____

Notes

True teaching is one that not teaches knowledge but stimulates children to gain it. Jill Eggleton

_____

_____

_____

_____

_____

_____

_____

_____

Daily Planner

Date: _____

To do

Morning _____

_____

_____

_____

_____

_____

_____

_____

_____

Afternoon _____

_____

_____

_____

_____

_____

_____

Evening _____

_____

_____

_____

_____

_____

_____

Goals

_____

_____

_____

_____

_____

Appointments

_____

_____

Call / Email

_____

_____

Meal Planner

_____

_____

Water Intake

◯ ◯ ◯ ◯
◯ ◯ ◯ ◯

Steps _____

Notes

No matter how good teaching may be, each student
must take the responsibility for his own education.
John Carolus

_____

_____

_____

_____

_____

_____

Daily Planner

Date: _____

To do

Morning _____
_____
_____
_____
_____
_____
_____
_____

Afternoon _____
_____
_____
_____
_____
_____
_____

Evening _____
_____
_____
_____
_____
_____
_____

Goals
_____
_____
_____
_____
_____

Appointments
_____
_____

Call / Email
_____
_____

Meal Planner
_____
_____

Water Intake
○ ○ ○ ○
○ ○ ○ ○

Steps _____

Notes

All I am saying in this book can be summed up in two words: Trust Children. Nothing could be more simple, or more difficult. Difficult because to trust children we must first learn to trust ourselves, and most of us were taught as children that we could not be trusted. John Holt
_____
_____
_____
_____
_____

Daily Planner

Date: _____

To do

Morning _____

_____
_____
_____
_____
_____
_____
_____

Afternoon _____

_____
_____
_____
_____
_____
_____

Evening _____

_____
_____
_____
_____
_____
_____

Goals

_____
_____
_____
_____
_____

Appointments

_____
_____
_____

Call / Email

_____
_____
_____

Meal Planner

_____
_____
_____

Water Intake

○ ○ ○ ○
○ ○ ○ ○

Steps _____

Notes

"Education is evolving due to the impact of the Internet. We cannot teach our students in the same manner in which we were taught. Change is necessary to engage students not in the curriculum we are responsible for teaching, but in school. Period." April Chamberlain

_____
_____
_____
_____
_____

workout log

Week

Date: [   ] Time: [   ] Week: [   ]

Weight

| Workout Day : | ① | ② | ③ | ④ | ⑤ | ⑥ | ⑦ |

Exercise	Reps	Set -1	Set -2	Set -3	Set -4	Set -5

Body Fat

Chest

Right Arm

Left Arm

Date: [   ] Time: [   ] Week: [   ]

Waist

| Workout Day : | ① | ② | ③ | ④ | ⑤ | ⑥ | ⑦ |

Exercise	Reps	Set -1	Set -2	Set -3	Set -4	Set -5

Hips

Right Leg

Left Leg

To Do List This Week

Day _____

Date & Month _____

No.	To Do	Yes/No	
_____	_____	☐	☐
_____	_____	☐	☐
_____	_____	☐	☐
_____	_____	☐	☐
_____	_____	☐	☐
_____	_____	☐	☐
_____	_____	☐	☐
_____	_____	☐	☐
_____	_____	☐	☐
_____	_____	☐	☐
_____	_____	☐	☐
_____	_____	☐	☐
_____	_____	☐	☐
_____	_____	☐	☐
_____	_____	☐	☐
_____	_____	☐	☐
_____	_____	☐	☐
_____	_____	☐	☐
_____	_____	☐	☐
_____	_____	☐	☐

Notes _____

_____

_____

_____

Daily Planner

Date: _____

To do

Morning _____

_____

_____

_____

_____

_____

_____

_____

_____

Afternoon _____

_____

_____

_____

_____

_____

_____

_____

Evening _____

_____

_____

_____

_____

_____

_____

Goals

_____

_____

_____

_____

_____

Appointments

_____

_____

Call / Email

_____

_____

Meal Planner

_____

_____

Water Intake

◯ ◯ ◯ ◯
◯ ◯ ◯ ◯

Steps _____

Notes

No use to shout at them to pay attention. If the situations, the materials, the problems before the child do not interest him, his attention will slip off to what does interest him, and no amount of exhortation of threats will bring it back.

John Holt

_____

_____

_____

_____

_____

_____

Daily Planner

Date: _____

To do

Morning _____

_____

_____

_____

_____

_____

_____

_____

Afternoon _____

_____

_____

_____

_____

_____

_____

_____

Evening _____

_____

_____

_____

_____

_____

_____

Goals

_____

_____

_____

_____

_____

Appointments

_____

_____

Call / Email

_____

_____

Meal Planner

_____

_____

Water Intake

○ ○ ○
○ ○ ○

Steps _____

Notes

The important thing is not so much that every child should be taught, as that every child should be given the wish to learn. John Lubbock

_____

_____

_____

_____

_____

_____

_____

_____

Daily Planner

Date: _____

To do

Morning _____

_____

_____

_____

_____

_____

_____

Afternoon _____

_____

_____

_____

_____

_____

_____

Evening _____

_____

_____

_____

_____

_____

_____

Goals

_____

_____

_____

_____

Appointments

_____

_____

Call / Email

_____

_____

Meal Planner

_____

_____

Water Intake

◯ ◯ ◯ ◯
◯ ◯ ◯ ◯

Steps _____

Notes

Much education today is monumentally ineffective. All too often we are giving young people cut flowers when we should be teaching them to grow their own plants. John W. Gardner

_____

_____

_____

_____

_____

_____

_____

Daily Planner

Date: _____

To do

Morning _____

_____

_____

_____

_____

_____

_____

_____

Afternoon _____

_____

_____

_____

_____

_____

_____

_____

Evening _____

_____

_____

_____

_____

_____

_____

Goals

_____

_____

_____

_____

_____

Appointments

_____

_____

_____

Call / Email

_____

_____

_____

Meal Planner

_____

_____

_____

Water Intake

◯ ◯ ◯ ◯
◯ ◯ ◯ ◯

Steps _____

Notes

Learning is not the product of teaching. Learning is the product of the activity of learners. John Holt

_____

_____

_____

_____

_____

_____

_____

Daily Planner

Date: _____

To do

Morning _____

_____
_____
_____
_____
_____
_____
_____

Afternoon _____

_____
_____
_____
_____
_____

Evening _____

_____
_____
_____
_____
_____
_____

Goals

_____
_____
_____
_____
_____

Appointments

_____
_____

Call / Email

_____
_____

Meal Planner

_____
_____

Water Intake

◯ ◯ ◯ ◯
◯ ◯ ◯ ◯

Steps _____

Notes

The job of an educator is to teach students to see the vitality in themselves. Joseph Campbell

_____
_____
_____
_____
_____
_____
_____
_____

Daily Planner

Date: _____

To do

Morning _____

_____

_____

_____

_____

_____

_____

_____

Afternoon _____

_____

_____

_____

_____

_____

_____

_____

Evening _____

_____

_____

_____

_____

_____

_____

Goals

_____

_____

_____

_____

_____

Appointments

_____

_____

Call / Email

_____

_____

Meal Planner

_____

_____

Water Intake

○ ○ ○ ○
○ ○ ○ ○

Steps _____

Notes

Education is a private matter between the person and the world of knowledge and experience and has little to do with school or college. Lillian Smith

_____

_____

_____

_____

_____

_____

_____

Daily Planner

Date: _____

To do

Morning _____

_____

_____

_____

_____

_____

_____

_____

_____

Afternoon _____

_____

_____

_____

_____

_____

_____

_____

Evening _____

_____

_____

_____

_____

_____

_____

Goals

_____

_____

_____

_____

_____

Appointments

_____

_____

_____

Call / Email

_____

_____

_____

Meal Planner

_____

_____

Water Intake

◯ ◯ ◯ ◯
◯ ◯ ◯ ◯

Steps _____

Notes

We learn more by looking for the answer to a question and not finding it than we do from learning the answer itself. Lord Alexander

_____

_____

_____

_____

_____

_____

_____

_____

MY MEETING NOTES

MEETING NAME & DATE -

ATTENDEES -

NEXT STEPS / DEADLINES -

MEETING NOTES -

You will not reap the fruit of individuality in your children if you
clone their education. Marilyn Howshall

MY MEETING NOTES

MEETING NAME & DATE -

ATTENDEES -

NEXT STEPS / DEADLINES -

MEETING NOTES -

_____
_____
_____
_____
_____
_____
_____
_____
_____
_____
_____
_____
_____
_____
_____
_____
_____
_____

"Whatever we believe about ourselves and our ability comes true for us." —Susan L. Taylor

MY MEETING NOTES

MEETING NAME & DATE -

ATTENDEES -

NEXT STEPS / DEADLINES -

MEETING NOTES -

_____

_____

_____

_____

_____

_____

_____

_____

_____

_____

_____

_____

_____

_____

_____

_____

_____

"I realized that beauty was not a thing that I could acquire or consume, it was something I just had to be." —Lupita Nyong'o

MY MEETING NOTES

MEETING NAME & DATE -

ATTENDEES -

NEXT STEPS / DEADLINES -

MEETING NOTES -

_____

_____

_____

_____

_____

_____

_____

_____

_____

_____

_____

_____

_____

_____

_____

_____

_____

_____

"Not everything that is faced can be changed, but nothing can be changed until it is faced."
James Baldwin

MY MEETING NOTES

_____

MEETING NAME & DATE -

ATTENDEES -

NEXT STEPS / DEADLINES -

MEETING NOTES -

_____

_____

_____

_____

_____

_____

_____

_____

_____

_____

_____

_____

_____

_____

_____

_____

_____

_____

_____

**The most common way people give up their power is by thinking
they don't have any. Alice Walker**

MY MEETING NOTES

MEETING NAME & DATE -

ATTENDEES -

NEXT STEPS / DEADLINES -

MEETING NOTES -

_____

_____

_____

_____

_____

_____

_____

_____

_____

_____

_____

_____

_____

_____

_____

_____

_____

_____

"The best way to not feel hopeless is to get up and do something. Don't wait for good things to happen to you. If you go out and make some good things happen, you will fill the world with hope, you will fill yourself with hope." —Barack Obama

MY MEETING NOTES

MEETING NAME & DATE -

ATTENDEES -

NEXT STEPS / DEADLINES -

MEETING NOTES -

_____
_____
_____
_____
_____
_____
_____
_____
_____
_____
_____
_____
_____
_____
_____
_____
_____
_____

"I use my platform for more than just myself. Art is a reflection of human emotions. To neglect the political is to neglect what essentially is your job of storytelling. I would rather be known for the content of my character than for the project that I did." —Zendaya

MY MEETING NOTES

MEETING NAME & DATE -

ATTENDEES -

NEXT STEPS / DEADLINES -

MEETING NOTES -

_____
_____
_____
_____
_____
_____
_____
_____
_____
_____
_____
_____
_____
_____
_____
_____
_____
_____
_____

"It is so liberating to really know what I want, what truly makes me happy, what I will not tolerate. I have learned that it is no one else's job to take care of me but me." —Beyoncé

MY MEETING NOTES

MEETING NAME & DATE -

ATTENDEES -

NEXT STEPS / DEADLINES -

MEETING NOTES -

_____

_____

_____

_____

_____

_____

_____

_____

_____

_____

_____

_____

_____

_____

_____

_____

_____

_____

"Hate is too great a burden to bear. It injures the hater more than it injures the hated."
Coretta Scott King

MY MEETING NOTES

MEETING NAME & DATE -

ATTENDEES -

NEXT STEPS / DEADLINES -

MEETING NOTES -

_____
_____
_____
_____
_____
_____
_____
_____
_____
_____
_____
_____
_____
_____
_____
_____
_____
_____
_____

"When you put love out in the world it travels, and it can touch people and reach people in ways that we never even expected." —Laverne Cox

MY MEETING NOTES

MEETING NAME & DATE -

ATTENDEES -

NEXT STEPS / DEADLINES -

MEETING NOTES -

_____

_____

_____

_____

_____

_____

_____

_____

_____

_____

_____

_____

_____

_____

_____

_____

_____

_____

_____

"I love my body, and I would never change anything about it. I'm not asking you to like my body. I'm just asking you to let me be me." —Serena Williams

MY MEETING NOTES

MEETING NAME & DATE -

ATTENDEES -

NEXT STEPS / DEADLINES -

MEETING NOTES -

_____
_____
_____
_____
_____
_____
_____
_____
_____
_____
_____
_____
_____
_____
_____
_____
_____
_____
_____

"Dreams are lovely but they are just dreams. Fleeting, ephemeral, pretty. But dreams do not come true just because you dream them. It's hard work that makes things happen. It's hard work that creates change." —Shonda Rhimes

MONTHLY REVIEW

MONTH OF

THIS MONTH I ACHIEVED

_____
_____
_____
_____
_____
_____
_____
_____

WHAT WORKED

_____
_____
_____
_____

WHAT DIDN'T WORK

_____
_____
_____
_____

DO MORE OF	DO LESS OF

MONTHLY REVIEW

MONTH OF

THIS MONTH I ACHIEVED

_____

_____

_____

_____

_____

_____

_____

_____

_____

WHAT WORKED

_____

_____

_____

_____

WHAT DIDN'T WORK

_____

_____

_____

_____

DO MORE OF

DO LESS OF

APRIL

MON
LEGS

Stretching and warm-up
25 Squats
25 Sumo Squats
Repeat above March in place for 20 sec
Stretch muscles
Relax

TUES
ABS

Stretching and warm-up
20 Standing Oblique Twists
30-second Floor Plank
Repeat above
March in place for 20 seconds
Stretch muscles
Relax

WED
ARMS

Stretching and warm-up
25 Push-ups
20 Wall Tricep Pushes
Repeat above
March in place for 20 seconds
Stretch muscles
Relax

THURS
CARDIO

Stretching and warm-up
50 Jumping Jacks
30-second Sprint in place
Repeat above
March in place for 20 seconds
Stretch muscles
Relax

FRI
COMBO

Stretching and warm-up
10 Squats & 10 Sumo Squats
10 Standing Oblique Twists
March in place for 20 seconds
20 Push-ups
25 Jumping Jacks
March in place for 20 seconds
Stretch muscles
Relax

SAT
YOUR PICK

Choose from Day 1-4
to work on your chosen area:
Legs
Abs
Arms or
Cardio

SUN
REST

Take a break!
You deserve it.

workout log

Week

Date : _____ Time : _____ Week : _____

Workout Day : ① ② ③ ④ ⑤ ⑥ ⑦

Exercise	Reps	Set -1	Set -2	Set -3	Set -4	Set -5

Date : _____ Time : _____ Week : _____

Workout Day : ① ② ③ ④ ⑤ ⑥ ⑦

Exercise	Reps	Set -1	Set -2	Set -3	Set -4	Set -5

Weight

Body Fat

Chest

Right Arm

Left Arm

Waist

Hips

Right Leg

Left Leg

THIS MONTH'S LIST

Month: April Year: _____

Potential Items to Plan/Schedule:

District Board Mtg
District Principal Mtg
Campus Admin Mtg
Vertical Team Mtg
Parent Conferences
LPACs/ELLs/ARDs
Progress Reports/Report Cards
Master Schedule Review
Team Leader/Dept. Chair Mtg
Professional Learning Community (PLC) Mtg
Athletic Event Admin Coverage Schedule
Teachers I need to meet with (observe/walkthrough)

Potential Assessments

Campus Level Assessments-State Aligned Objectives

Additions

Shared Decision Making Council (SDMC)
Picture Day Planning
State Testing Planning & Roster Development

_____

_____

_____

_____

_____

_____

_____

_____

_____

_____

_____

MONTHLY PLANNER
MONTH: _____

MONDAY	TUESDAY	WEDNESDAY	THURSDAY	FRIDAY	SATURDAY	SUNDAY

PRIORITY

Daily Planner

Date: _____

To do

Morning _____
_____
_____
_____
_____
_____
_____
_____

Afternoon _____
_____
_____
_____
_____
_____
_____
_____

Evening _____
_____
_____
_____
_____
_____
_____

Goals

_____
_____
_____
_____
_____

Appointments

_____
_____

Call / Email

_____
_____

Meal Planner

_____
_____

Water Intake

◯ ◯ ◯ ◯
◯ ◯ ◯ ◯

Steps _____

Notes

No use to shout at them to pay attention. If the situations, the materials, the problems before the child do not interest him, his attention will slip off to what does interest him, and no amount of exhortation of threats will bring it back. John Holt

_____
_____
_____
_____
_____

Daily Planner

Date: _____

To do

Morning _____
_____
_____
_____
_____
_____
_____
_____

Afternoon _____
_____
_____
_____
_____
_____
_____

Evening _____
_____
_____
_____
_____
_____
_____

Goals

_____
_____
_____
_____

Appointments

_____
_____

Call / Email

_____
_____

Meal Planner

_____
_____

Water Intake

◯ ◯ ◯ ◯
◯ ◯ ◯ ◯

Steps _____

Notes

The important thing is not so much that every child should be taught, as that every child should be given the wish to learn. John Lubbock

_____
_____
_____
_____
_____
_____
_____

Daily Planner

Date: _____

To do

Morning _____

_____

_____

_____

_____

_____

_____

_____

Afternoon _____

_____

_____

_____

_____

_____

_____

Evening _____

_____

_____

_____

_____

_____

_____

Goals

_____

_____

_____

_____

_____

Appointments

_____

_____

Call / Email

_____

_____

Meal Planner

_____

_____

Water Intake

◯ ◯ ◯

◯ ◯ ◯

Steps _____

Notes

Much education today is monumentally ineffective.
All too often we are giving young people cut flowers
when we should be teaching them to grow their
own plants. John W. Gardner

_____

_____

_____

_____

_____

_____

Daily Planner

Date: _____

To do

Morning _____

_____

_____

_____

_____

_____

_____

_____

_____

Afternoon _____

_____

_____

_____

_____

_____

_____

Evening _____

_____

_____

_____

_____

_____

_____

Goals

_____

_____

_____

_____

_____

Appointments

_____

_____

Call / Email

_____

_____

Meal Planner

_____

_____

Water Intake

◯ ◯ ◯ ◯
◯ ◯ ◯ ◯

Steps _____

Notes

Learning is not the product of teaching. Learning is the product of the activity of learners. John Holt

_____

_____

_____

_____

_____

_____

Date: _____

To do
_____
Morning _____
_____
_____
_____
_____
_____
_____

Afternoon _____
_____
_____
_____
_____
_____
_____
_____

Evening _____
_____
_____
_____
_____
_____
_____

Goals
_____
_____
_____
_____
_____

Appointments
_____
_____
_____

Call / Email
_____
_____
_____

Meal Planner
_____
_____
_____

Water Intake
◯ ◯ ◯ ◯
◯ ◯ ◯ ◯

Steps _____

Notes
The job of an educator is to teach students to see the vitality in themselves. Joseph Campbell
_____
_____
_____
_____
_____
_____
_____

Date: _____

To do

Morning _____

_____

_____

_____

_____

_____

_____

Afternoon _____

_____

_____

_____

_____

_____

_____

Evening _____

_____

_____

_____

_____

_____

Goals

_____

_____

_____

_____

Appointments

_____

_____

Call / Email

_____

_____

Meal Planner

_____

_____

Water Intake

◯ ◯ ◯ ◯
◯ ◯ ◯ ◯

Steps _____

Notes

Education is a private matter between the person and the world of knowledge and experience and has little to do with school or college. Lillian Smith

_____

_____

_____

_____

_____

_____

_____

Date: _____

To do

Morning _____

_____

_____

_____

_____

_____

_____

_____

Afternoon _____

_____

_____

_____

_____

_____

_____

Evening _____

_____

_____

_____

_____

_____

_____

Goals

_____

_____

_____

_____

_____

Appointments

_____

_____

Call / Email

_____

_____

Meal Planner

_____

_____

Water Intake

◯ ◯ ◯ ◯
◯ ◯ ◯ ◯

Steps _____

Notes

We learn more by looking for the answer to a question and not finding it than we do from learning the answer itself. Lord Alexander

_____

_____

_____

_____

_____

_____

_____

_____

workout log

Week

Date : _____ Time : _____ Week : _____

Workout Day : ① ② ③ ④ ⑤ ⑥ ⑦

Exercise	Reps	Set-1	Set-2	Set-3	Set-4	Set-5

Date : _____ Time : _____ Week : _____

Workout Day : ① ② ③ ④ ⑤ ⑥ ⑦

Exercise	Reps	Set-1	Set-2	Set-3	Set-4	Set-5

Weight

Body Fat

Chest

Right Arm

Left Arm

Waist

Hips

Right Leg

Left Leg

To Do List This Week

Day _____

Date & Month _____

No.	To Do	Yes/No	
____	_____	☐	☐
____	_____	☐	☐
____	_____	☐	☐
____	_____	☐	☐
____	_____	☐	☐
____	_____	☐	☐
____	_____	☐	☐
____	_____	☐	☐
____	_____	☐	☐
____	_____	☐	☐
____	_____	☐	☐
____	_____	☐	☐
____	_____	☐	☐
____	_____	☐	☐
____	_____	☐	☐
____	_____	☐	☐
____	_____	☐	☐
____	_____	☐	☐
____	_____	☐	☐
____	_____	☐	☐

Notes _____

_____

_____

_____

Date: _____

To do

Morning _____

_____

_____

_____

_____

_____

_____

_____

Afternoon _____

_____

_____

_____

_____

_____

_____

_____

Evening _____

_____

_____

_____

_____

_____

_____

Goals

_____

_____

_____

_____

_____

Appointments

_____

_____

_____

Call / Email

_____

_____

_____

Meal Planner

_____

_____

_____

Water Intake

○ ○ ○ ○
○ ○ ○ ○

Steps _____

Notes

You will not reap the fruit of individuality in your children if you clone their education.
Marilyn Howshall

_____

_____

_____

_____

_____

_____

_____

Daily Planner

Date: _____

To do

Morning _____

_____

_____

_____

_____

_____

_____

Afternoon _____

_____

_____

_____

_____

_____

_____

Evening _____

_____

_____

_____

_____

_____

_____

Goals

_____

_____

_____

_____

Appointments

_____

_____

Call / Email

_____

_____

Meal Planner

_____

_____

Water Intake

○ ○ ○ ○
○ ○ ○ ○

Steps _____

Notes

A man's mind, stretched by new ideas, may never return to its original dimensions. Oliver Wendell Holmes Jr.

_____

_____

_____

_____

_____

_____

_____

Daily Planner

Date: _____

To do

Morning _____

_____

_____

_____

_____

_____

_____

_____

Afternoon _____

_____

_____

_____

_____

_____

_____

Evening _____

_____

_____

_____

_____

_____

_____

Goals

_____

_____

_____

_____

_____

Appointments

_____

_____

Call / Email

_____

_____

Meal Planner

_____

_____

Water Intake

◯ ◯ ◯ ◯
◯ ◯ ◯ ◯

Steps _____

Notes

Never let formal education get in the way of your learning. Mark Twain

_____

_____

_____

_____

_____

_____

_____

Date: _____

To do

Morning _____

_____

_____

_____

_____

_____

_____

_____

Afternoon _____

_____

_____

_____

_____

_____

_____

_____

Evening _____

_____

_____

_____

_____

_____

_____

_____

Goals

_____

_____

_____

_____

_____

Appointments

_____

_____

_____

Call / Email

_____

_____

_____

Meal Planner

_____

_____

Water Intake

◯ ◯ ◯ ◯
◯ ◯ ◯ ◯

Steps _____

Notes

Through education comes understanding. Through understanding comes true appreciation. All children are artists. The problem is how to remain an artist once he grows up. - Pablo Picasso

_____

_____

_____

_____

_____

_____

Daily Planner

Date: _____

To do

Morning _____

_____

_____

_____

_____

_____

_____

_____

_____

Afternoon _____

_____

_____

_____

_____

_____

_____

Evening _____

_____

_____

_____

_____

_____

_____

Goals

_____

_____

_____

_____

Appointments

_____

_____

_____

Call / Email

_____

_____

_____

Meal Planner

_____

_____

Water Intake

○ ○ ○ ○
○ ○ ○ ○

Steps _____

Notes

A master can tell you what he expects of you. A teacher, though, awakens your own expectations.
Patricia Neal

_____

_____

_____

_____

_____

_____

_____

_____

Daily Planner

Date: _____

To do

Morning _____

_____

_____

_____

_____

_____

_____

_____

Afternoon _____

_____

_____

_____

_____

_____

_____

Evening _____

_____

_____

_____

_____

_____

Goals

_____

_____

_____

_____

_____

Appointments

_____

_____

Call / Email

_____

_____

Meal Planner

_____

_____

Water Intake

○ ○ ○ ○
○ ○ ○ ○

Steps _____

Notes

Our schools have a doubly hard task, not just improving reading, writing and arithmetic but entrepreneurship, innovation, and creativity. Ken Robinson

_____

_____

_____

_____

_____

_____

_____

Daily Planner

Date: _____

To do

Morning _____
_____
_____
_____
_____
_____
_____
_____

Afternoon _____
_____
_____
_____
_____
_____
_____
_____

Evening _____
_____
_____
_____
_____
_____
_____

Goals
_____
_____
_____
_____
_____

Appointments
_____
_____
_____

Call / Email
_____
_____
_____

Meal Planner
_____
_____
_____

Water Intake
○ ○ ○ ○
○ ○ ○ ○

Steps _____

Notes

Don't limit a child to your own learning, for he was born in another time. Rabbinical Saying

_____
_____
_____
_____
_____
_____
_____

workout log

Week

Date : [_____]   Time : [_____]   Week: [_____]

Workout Day : ① ② ③ ④ ⑤ ⑥ ⑦

Exercise	Reps	Set -1	Set -2	Set -3	Set -4	Set -5

Date : [_____]   Time : [_____]   Week: [_____]

Workout Day : ① ② ③ ④ ⑤ ⑥ ⑦

Exercise	Reps	Set -1	Set -2	Set -3	Set -4	Set -5

Weight

Body Fat

Chest

Right Arm

Left Arm

Waist

Hips

Right Leg

Left Leg

To Do List This Week

Day _____

Date & Month _____

No.	To Do	Yes/No	
___	_____	☐	☐
___	_____	☐	☐
___	_____	☐	☐
___	_____	☐	☐
___	_____	☐	☐
___	_____	☐	☐
___	_____	☐	☐
___	_____	☐	☐
___	_____	☐	☐
___	_____	☐	☐
___	_____	☐	☐
___	_____	☐	☐
___	_____	☐	☐
___	_____	☐	☐
___	_____	☐	☐
___	_____	☐	☐
___	_____	☐	☐
___	_____	☐	☐
___	_____	☐	☐
___	_____	☐	☐

Notes _____

_____

_____

_____

Daily Planner

Date: _____

To do

Morning _____
_____
_____
_____
_____
_____
_____
_____

Afternoon _____
_____
_____
_____
_____
_____
_____

Evening _____
_____
_____
_____
_____
_____

Goals
_____
_____
_____
_____
_____

Appointments
_____
_____

Call / Email
_____
_____

Meal Planner
_____
_____

Water Intake
◯ ◯ ◯ ◯
◯ ◯ ◯ ◯

Steps _____

Notes

"It is not about the technology; it's about sharing knowledge and information, communicating efficiently, building learning communities and creating a culture of professionalism in schools. These are the key responsibilities of all educational leaders". Marion Ginapolis
_____
_____
_____
_____
_____

Daily Planner

Date: _____

To do

Morning _____

_____

_____

_____

_____

_____

_____

_____

Afternoon _____

_____

_____

_____

_____

_____

_____

_____

Evening _____

_____

_____

_____

_____

_____

_____

Goals

_____

_____

_____

_____

_____

Appointments

_____

_____

_____

Call / Email

_____

_____

_____

Meal Planner

_____

_____

Water Intake

◯ ◯ ◯ ◯
◯ ◯ ◯ ◯

Steps _____

Notes

If the education and studies of children were suited to their inclinations and capacities, many would be made useful members of society that otherwise would make no figure in it. Samuel Richardson

_____

_____

_____

_____

_____

_____

Daily Planner

Date: _____

To do

Morning _____

_____

_____

_____

_____

_____

_____

_____

Afternoon _____

_____

_____

_____

_____

_____

_____

_____

Evening _____

_____

_____

_____

_____

_____

_____

Goals

_____

_____

_____

_____

Appointments

_____

_____

Call / Email

_____

_____

Meal Planner

_____

_____

Water Intake

◯ ◯ ◯

◯ ◯ ◯

Steps _____

Notes

I cannot teach anybody anything, I can only make them think. Socrates

_____

_____

_____

_____

_____

Daily Planner

Date: _____

To do

Morning _____

_____

_____

_____

_____

_____

_____

_____

Afternoon _____

_____

_____

_____

_____

_____

_____

Evening _____

_____

_____

_____

_____

_____

Goals

_____

_____

_____

_____

Appointments

_____

_____

Call / Email

_____

_____

Meal Planner

_____

_____

Water Intake

◯ ◯ ◯ ◯
◯ ◯ ◯ ◯

Steps _____

Notes

One learns by doing a thing; for though you think
you know it, you have no certainty until you try.
Sophocles

_____

_____

_____

_____

_____

_____

_____

_____

Daily Planner

Date: _____

To do

Morning _____

_____

_____

_____

_____

_____

_____

Afternoon _____

_____

_____

_____

_____

_____

Evening _____

_____

_____

_____

_____

_____

Goals

_____

_____

_____

_____

_____

Appointments

_____

_____

Call / Email

_____

_____

Meal Planner

_____

_____

Water Intake

○ ○ ○ ○
○ ○ ○ ○

Steps _____

Notes

A teacher is one who makes himself progressively unnecessary. Thomas Carruthers

_____

_____

_____

_____

_____

_____

Daily Planner

Date: _____

To do

Morning _____

_____

_____

_____

_____

_____

_____

_____

Afternoon _____

_____

_____

_____

_____

_____

_____

_____

Evening _____

_____

_____

_____

_____

_____

_____

Goals

_____

_____

_____

_____

_____

Appointments

_____

_____

Call / Email

_____

_____

Meal Planner

_____

_____

Water Intake

◯ ◯ ◯

◯ ◯ ◯

Steps _____

Notes

An education isn't how much you have committed to memory, or even how much you know. It's being able to differentiate between what you do know and what you don't. It's knowing where to go to find out what you need to know; and it's knowing how to use the information you get. William Feather

_____

_____

_____

_____

Daily Planner

Date: _____

To do

Morning _____
_____
_____
_____
_____
_____
_____
_____

Afternoon _____
_____
_____
_____
_____
_____
_____

Evening _____
_____
_____
_____
_____
_____
_____
_____

Goals
_____
_____
_____
_____
_____

Appointments
_____
_____

Call / Email
_____
_____

Meal Planner
_____
_____

Water Intake

◯ ◯ ◯ ◯
◯ ◯ ◯ ◯

Steps _____

Notes
The rule for every man is, not to depend on the education which other men have prepared for him —not even to consent to it; but to strive to see things as they are, and to be himself as he is. Defeat lies in self-surrender. Woodrow Wilson

_____
_____
_____
_____
_____
_____

workout log

Week

Date : _____ Time : _____ Week : _____

Workout Day : ① ② ③ ④ ⑤ ⑥ ⑦

Exercise	Reps	Set - 1	Set - 2	Set - 3	Set - 4	Set - 5

Date : _____ Time : _____ Week : _____

Workout Day : ① ② ③ ④ ⑤ ⑥ ⑦

Exercise	Reps	Set - 1	Set - 2	Set - 3	Set - 4	Set - 5

Weight

Body Fat

Chest

Right Arm

Left Arm

Waist

Hips

Right Leg

Left Leg

To Do List This Week

Day _____

Date & Month _____

No.	To Do	Yes/No	
___	_____	☐	☐
___	_____	☐	☐
___	_____	☐	☐
___	_____	☐	☐
___	_____	☐	☐
___	_____	☐	☐
___	_____	☐	☐
___	_____	☐	☐
___	_____	☐	☐
___	_____	☐	☐
___	_____	☐	☐
___	_____	☐	☐
___	_____	☐	☐
___	_____	☐	☐
___	_____	☐	☐
___	_____	☐	☐
___	_____	☐	☐
___	_____	☐	☐
___	_____	☐	☐
___	_____	☐	☐
___	_____	☐	☐

Notes _____

_____

_____

_____

Daily Planner

Date: _____

To do

Morning _____
_____
_____
_____
_____
_____
_____
_____

Afternoon _____
_____
_____
_____
_____
_____

Evening _____
_____
_____
_____
_____
_____
_____

Goals
_____
_____
_____
_____
_____

Appointments
_____
_____
_____

Call / Email
_____
_____
_____

Meal Planner
_____
_____
_____

Water Intake
◯ ◯ ◯ ◯
◯ ◯ ◯ ◯

Steps _____

Notes
Tell me and I forget, teach me and I may remember,
involve me and I learn. Benjamin Franklin
_____
_____
_____
_____
_____
_____
_____

Daily Planner

Date: _____

To do

Morning _____

_____

_____

_____

_____

_____

_____

_____

Afternoon _____

_____

_____

_____

_____

_____

_____

Evening _____

_____

_____

_____

_____

_____

_____

Goals

_____

_____

_____

_____

_____

Appointments

_____

_____

Call / Email

_____

_____

Meal Planner

_____

_____

Water Intake

○ ○ ○ ○
○ ○ ○ ○

Steps _____

Notes

I am not a teacher, but an awakener. Robert Frost

_____

_____

_____

_____

_____

_____

Daily Planner

Date: _____

To do

Morning _____

_____

_____

_____

_____

_____

_____

_____

Afternoon _____

_____

_____

_____

_____

_____

_____

Evening _____

_____

_____

_____

_____

_____

_____

Goals

_____

_____

_____

_____

_____

Appointments

_____

_____

_____

Call / Email

_____

_____

_____

Meal Planner

_____

_____

Water Intake

○ ○ ○ ○
○ ○ ○ ○

Steps _____

Notes

Spoon feeding in the long run teaches us nothing but the shape of the spoon. E.M. Forster

_____

_____

_____

_____

_____

_____

_____

Daily Planner

Date: _____

To do

Morning _____

_____

_____

_____

_____

_____

_____

_____

Afternoon _____

_____

_____

_____

_____

_____

Evening _____

_____

_____

_____

_____

_____

Goals

_____

_____

_____

_____

_____

Appointments

_____

_____

_____

Call / Email

_____

_____

_____

Meal Planner

_____

_____

Water Intake

◯ ◯ ◯ ◯
◯ ◯ ◯ ◯

Steps _____

Notes

"I have a dream that my four little children will one day live in a nation where they will not be judged by the color of their skin, but by the content of their character." —Martin Luther King, Jr.

_____

_____

_____

_____

_____

_____

_____

Daily Planner

Date: _____

To do

Morning _____

_____

_____

_____

_____

_____

_____

_____

Afternoon _____

_____

_____

_____

_____

_____

_____

_____

Evening _____

_____

_____

_____

_____

_____

_____

Goals

_____

_____

_____

_____

_____

Appointments

_____

_____

Call / Email

_____

_____

Meal Planner

_____

_____

Water Intake

◯ ◯ ◯ ◯
◯ ◯ ◯ ◯

Steps _____

Notes

"There is nothing like returning to a place that remains unchanged to find the ways in which you yourself have altered." —Nelson Mandela

_____

_____

_____

_____

_____

_____

_____

Date: _____

To do

Morning _____

_____

_____

_____

_____

_____

_____

_____

Afternoon _____

_____

_____

_____

_____

_____

_____

Evening _____

_____

_____

_____

_____

_____

_____

Goals

_____

_____

_____

_____

_____

Appointments

_____

_____

Call / Email

_____

_____

Meal Planner

_____

_____

Water Intake

◯ ◯ ◯ ◯
◯ ◯ ◯ ◯

Steps _____

Notes

"Don't try to lessen yourself for the world; let the world catch up to you." —Beyoncé

_____

_____

_____

_____

_____

_____

_____

Daily Planner

Date: _____

To do

Morning _____
_____
_____
_____
_____
_____
_____
_____

Afternoon _____
_____
_____
_____
_____
_____
_____
_____

Evening _____
_____
_____
_____
_____
_____
_____

Goals
_____
_____
_____
_____
_____

Appointments
_____
_____

Call / Email
_____
_____

Meal Planner
_____
_____

Water Intake
◯ ◯ ◯ ◯
◯ ◯ ◯ ◯

Steps _____

Notes
"I'm not concerned with your liking or disliking me... all I ask is that you respect me as a human being." —Jackie Robinson
_____
_____
_____
_____
_____
_____
_____

MY MEETING NOTES

MEETING NAME & DATE -

ATTENDEES -

NEXT STEPS / DEADLINES -

MEETING NOTES -

_____
_____
_____
_____
_____
_____
_____
_____
_____
_____
_____
_____
_____
_____
_____
_____
_____
_____
_____

"How far you go in life depends on your being tender with the young, compassionate with the aged, sympathetic with the striving, and tolerant of the weak and strong. Because someday in your life you will have been all of these. —George Washington Carver

MY MEETING NOTES

MEETING NAME & DATE -

ATTENDEES -

NEXT STEPS / DEADLINES -

MEETING NOTES -

_____

_____

_____

_____

_____

_____

_____

_____

_____

_____

_____

_____

_____

_____

_____

_____

_____

_____

_____

"You should never discount anything. I think so many of us tend to be comfortable with what we're not and complacent with what we're not. You really don't have to be. I didn't solve world peace or anything — it's not like that. But something that felt so small and intangible ended up being tangible. And that's just the coolest thing in the world." —Issa Rae

MY MEETING NOTES

MEETING NAME & DATE -

ATTENDEES -

NEXT STEPS / DEADLINES -

MEETING NOTES -

_____

_____

_____

_____

_____

_____

_____

_____

_____

_____

_____

_____

_____

_____

_____

_____

_____

_____

_____

Instead of letting your hardships and failures discourage or exhaust you, let them inspire you. Let them make you even hungrier to succeed. Michelle Obama

MY MEETING NOTES

MEETING NAME & DATE -

ATTENDEES -

NEXT STEPS / DEADLINES -

MEETING NOTES -

_____

_____

_____

_____

_____

_____

_____

_____

_____

_____

_____

_____

_____

_____

_____

_____

_____

_____

_____

_____

"If we can't look at the good, bad, and ugly of who we are, we are never going to progress as people— ever." —Rosie Perez

MY MEETING NOTES

MEETING NAME & DATE -

ATTENDEES -

NEXT STEPS / DEADLINES -

MEETING NOTES -

_____

_____

_____

_____

_____

_____

_____

_____

_____

_____

_____

_____

_____

_____

_____

_____

_____

_____

_____

_____

_____

"Bringing the gifts that my ancestors gave, I am the dream and the hope of the slave. I rise. I rise. I rise." —Maya Angelou

MY MEETING NOTES

MEETING NAME & DATE -

ATTENDEES -

NEXT STEPS / DEADLINES -

MEETING NOTES -

"Black people have always been America's wilderness in search of a promised land."
Cornel West

MY MEETING NOTES

MEETING NAME & DATE -

ATTENDEES -

NEXT STEPS / DEADLINES -

MEETING NOTES -

_____

_____

_____

_____

_____

_____

_____

_____

_____

_____

_____

_____

_____

_____

_____

_____

_____

_____

_____

"I don't have any time to stay up all night worrying about what someone who doesn't love me has to say about me." —Viola Davis

MY MEETING NOTES

MEETING NAME & DATE -

ATTENDEES -

NEXT STEPS / DEADLINES -

MEETING NOTES -

_____
_____
_____
_____
_____
_____
_____
_____
_____
_____
_____
_____
_____
_____
_____
_____
_____
_____
_____

"Identity is a prison you can never escape, but the way to redeem your past is not to run from it, but to try to understand it, and use it as a foundation to grow." —Jay-Z

MY MEETING NOTES

MEETING NAME & DATE -

ATTENDEES -

NEXT STEPS / DEADLINES -

MEETING NOTES -

"We all require and want respect, man or woman, black or white. It's our basic human right."
Aretha Franklin

MY MEETING NOTES

MEETING NAME & DATE -

ATTENDEES -

NEXT STEPS / DEADLINES -

MEETING NOTES -

"Never, ever, let them see you sweat, negra. Fight until you can't breathe, and if you have to forfeit, you forfeit smiling, make them think you let them win."
Elizabeth Acevedo, Clap When You Land

MY MEETING NOTES

MEETING NAME & DATE -

ATTENDEES -

NEXT STEPS / DEADLINES -

MEETING NOTES -

_____
_____
_____
_____
_____
_____
_____
_____
_____
_____
_____
_____
_____
_____
_____
_____
_____
_____
_____

"No hay que llorar/ Que la vida es un carnaval." (There's no need to cry. Life is a carnival.)
Celia Cruz

MY MEETING NOTES

MEETING NAME & DATE -

ATTENDEES -

NEXT STEPS / DEADLINES -

MEETING NOTES -

_____

_____

_____

_____

_____

_____

_____

_____

_____

_____

_____

_____

_____

_____

_____

_____

_____

_____

"I am not going to die; I'm going home like a shooting star." —Sojourner Truth

MONTHLY REVIEW

MONTH OF

THIS MONTH I ACHIEVED

_____

_____

_____

_____

_____

_____

_____

_____

_____

WHAT WORKED

_____

_____

_____

_____

WHAT DIDN'T WORK

_____

_____

_____

_____

DO MORE OF

DO LESS OF

MONTHLY REVIEW

THIS MONTH I ACHIEVED

_____
_____
_____
_____
_____
_____
_____
_____

WHAT WORKED

_____
_____
_____

WHAT DIDN'T WORK

_____
_____
_____

DO MORE OF

DO LESS OF

MAY

MON
LEGS

Stretching and warm-up
25 Squats
25 Sumo Squats
Repeat above March in place for 20 sec
Stretch muscles
Relax

TUES
ABS

Stretching and warm-up
20 Standing Oblique Twists
30-second Floor Plank
Repeat above
March in place for 20 seconds
Stretch muscles
Relax

WED
ARMS

Stretching and warm-up
25 Push-ups
20 Wall Tricep Pushes
Repeat above
March in place for 20
seconds
Stretch muscles
Relax

THURS
CARDIO

Stretching and warm-up
50 Jumping Jacks
30-second Sprint in place
Repeat above
March in place for 20
seconds
Stretch muscles
Relax

FRI
COMBO

Stretching and warm-up
10 Squats & 10 Sumo
Squats
10 Standing Oblique Twists
March in place for 20
seconds
20 Push-ups
25 Jumping Jacks
March in place for 20
seconds
Stretch muscles
Relax

SAT
YOUR PICK

Choose from Day 1-4
to work on your chosen area:
Legs
Abs
Arms or
Cardio

SUN
REST

Take a break!
You deserve it.

workout log

Week

Date: _____ Time: _____ Week: _____

Weight

Workout Day: ① ② ③ ④ ⑤ ⑥ ⑦

Exercise	Reps	Set -1	Set -2	Set -3	Set -4	Set -5

Body Fat

Chest

Right Arm

Left Arm

Date: _____ Time: _____ Week: _____

Waist

Workout Day: ① ② ③ ④ ⑤ ⑥ ⑦

Exercise	Reps	Set -1	Set -2	Set -3	Set -4	Set -5

Hips

Right Leg

Left Leg

THIS MONTH'S LIST

Month: May Year: _____

Potential Items to Plan/Schedule:
District Board Mtg
District Principal Mtg
Campus Admin Mtg
Vertical Team Mtg
Parent Conferences
LPACs/ELLs/ARDs
Progress Reports/Report Cards
Master Schedule Review
Team Leader/Dept. Chair Mtg
Professional Learning Community (PLC) Mtg
Athletic Event Admin Coverage Schedule
Teachers I need to meet with (observe/walkthrough)

Potential Assessments
Campus Level Assessments-State Aligned Objectives
High Frequency Word Assessment Gr. 1 & 2
AP & EOC Exams
State Assessment Administrations by Grade by Level

Additions
Shared Decision Making Council (SDMC)
Picture Day Planning
State Testing Planning & Roster Development
Graduation Event Planning
Summer School Preparation Planning
Promotion/Graduation Criteria Review

_____
_____
_____
_____
_____

MONTHLY PLANNER
MONTH: _____

MONDAY	TUESDAY	WEDNESDAY	THURSDAY	FRIDAY	SATURDAY	SUNDAY

PRIORITY

To Do List This Week

Day _____

Date & Month _____

No.	To Do	Yes/No
_____	_____	☐ ☐
_____	_____	☐ ☐
_____	_____	☐ ☐
_____	_____	☐ ☐
_____	_____	☐ ☐
_____	_____	☐ ☐
_____	_____	☐ ☐
_____	_____	☐ ☐
_____	_____	☐ ☐
_____	_____	☐ ☐
_____	_____	☐ ☐
_____	_____	☐ ☐
_____	_____	☐ ☐
_____	_____	☐ ☐
_____	_____	☐ ☐
_____	_____	☐ ☐
_____	_____	☐ ☐
_____	_____	☐ ☐
_____	_____	☐ ☐
_____	_____	☐ ☐

Notes _____
_____
_____
_____

Daily Planner

Date: _____

To do

Morning _____

_____

_____

_____

_____

_____

_____

_____

_____

Afternoon _____

_____

_____

_____

_____

_____

_____

Evening _____

_____

_____

_____

_____

_____

_____

_____

Goals

_____

_____

_____

_____

Appointments

_____

_____

Call / Email

_____

_____

Meal Planner

_____

_____

Water Intake

◯ ◯ ◯ ◯
◯ ◯ ◯ ◯

Steps _____

Notes

The mind is not a vessel to be filled, but a fire to be kindled. Plutarch

_____

_____

_____

_____

_____

_____

_____

Daily Planner

Date: _____

To do

Morning _____
_____
_____
_____
_____
_____
_____

Afternoon _____
_____
_____
_____
_____
_____
_____

Evening _____
_____
_____
_____
_____
_____
_____

Goals

_____
_____
_____
_____
_____

Appointments

_____
_____

Call / Email

_____
_____

Meal Planner

_____
_____

Water Intake

○ ○ ○
○ ○ ○

Steps _____

Notes

Do not train a child to learn by force or harshness;
but direct them to it by what amuses their minds, so
that you may be better able to discover with
accuracy the peculiar bent of the genius of each.
Plato

_____
_____
_____
_____
_____
_____

Daily Planner

Date: _____

To do

Morning _____
_____
_____
_____
_____
_____
_____
_____

Afternoon _____
_____
_____
_____
_____
_____
_____

Evening _____
_____
_____
_____
_____
_____
_____

Goals
_____
_____
_____
_____
_____

Appointments
_____
_____
_____

Call / Email
_____
_____
_____

Meal Planner
_____
_____
_____

Water Intake

◯ ◯ ◯ ◯
◯ ◯ ◯ ◯

Steps _____

Notes

What is a teacher? I'll tell you: it isn't someone who teaches something, but someone who inspires the student to give of her best in order to discover what she already knows. Paulo Coelho
_____
_____
_____
_____
_____
_____

Daily Planner

Date: _____

To do

Morning _____
_____
_____
_____
_____
_____
_____
_____

Afternoon _____
_____
_____
_____
_____
_____
_____
_____

Evening _____
_____
_____
_____
_____
_____
_____
_____

Goals

_____
_____
_____
_____
_____

Appointments

_____
_____
_____

Call / Email

_____
_____
_____

Meal Planner

_____
_____
_____

Water Intake

○ ○ ○ ○
○ ○ ○ ○

Steps _____

Notes

True education does not consist merely in the acquiring of a few facts of science, history, literature, or art, but in the development of character. David O. McKay

_____
_____
_____
_____
_____
_____
_____

Date: _____

To do

Morning _____

_____

_____

_____

_____

_____

_____

_____

Afternoon _____

_____

_____

_____

_____

_____

_____

Evening _____

_____

_____

_____

_____

_____

_____

Goals

_____

_____

_____

_____

_____

Appointments

_____

_____

Call / Email

_____

_____

Meal Planner

_____

_____

Water Intake

○ ○ ○ ○
○ ○ ○ ○

Steps _____

Notes

In learning you will teach, and in teaching you will learn. Phil Collins

_____

_____

_____

_____

_____

_____

_____

Daily Planner

Date: _____

To do

Morning _____

_____

_____

_____

_____

_____

_____

_____

Afternoon _____

_____

_____

_____

_____

_____

_____

Evening _____

_____

_____

_____

_____

_____

_____

Goals

_____

_____

_____

_____

_____

Appointments

_____

_____

Call / Email

_____

_____

Meal Planner

_____

_____

Water Intake

◯ ◯ ◯ ◯
◯ ◯ ◯ ◯

Steps _____

Notes

Live as if you were to die tomorrow. Learn as if you were to live forever. Mahatma Gandhi

_____

_____

_____

_____

_____

_____

Daily Planner

Date: _____

To do

Morning _____

_____
_____
_____
_____
_____
_____
_____

Afternoon _____

_____
_____
_____
_____
_____
_____

Evening _____

_____
_____
_____
_____
_____
_____
_____

Goals

_____
_____
_____
_____

Appointments

_____
_____

Call / Email

_____
_____

Meal Planner

_____
_____

Water Intake

◯ ◯ ◯ ◯
◯ ◯ ◯ ◯

Steps _____

Notes

You can never be overdressed or overeducated.
Oscar Wilde

_____
_____
_____
_____
_____
_____
_____
_____

MONTHLY PLANNER
MONTH: _____

MONDAY	TUESDAY	WEDNESDAY	THURSDAY	FRIDAY	SATURDAY	SUNDAY

PRIORITY

To Do List This Week

Day _____

Date & Month _____

No.	To Do	Yes/No
___	_____	☐ ☐
___	_____	☐ ☐
___	_____	☐ ☐
___	_____	☐ ☐
___	_____	☐ ☐
___	_____	☐ ☐
___	_____	☐ ☐
___	_____	☐ ☐
___	_____	☐ ☐
___	_____	☐ ☐
___	_____	☐ ☐
___	_____	☐ ☐
___	_____	☐ ☐
___	_____	☐ ☐
___	_____	☐ ☐
___	_____	☐ ☐
___	_____	☐ ☐
___	_____	☐ ☐
___	_____	☐ ☐

Notes _____

_____

_____

_____

Date: _____

To do

Morning _____

_____

_____

_____

_____

_____

_____

_____

_____

Afternoon _____

_____

_____

_____

_____

_____

_____

_____

Evening _____

_____

_____

_____

_____

_____

_____

_____

_____

Goals

_____

_____

_____

_____

_____

Appointments

_____

_____

_____

Call / Email

_____

_____

_____

Meal Planner

_____

_____

Water Intake

○ ○ ○ ○
○ ○ ○ ○

Steps _____

Notes

The task of the modern educator is not to cut down jungles, but to irrigate deserts. C.S. Lewis

_____

_____

_____

_____

_____

_____

_____

_____

Daily Planner

Date: _____

To do

Morning _____

_____

_____

_____

_____

_____

_____

_____

Afternoon _____

_____

_____

_____

_____

_____

_____

Evening _____

_____

_____

_____

_____

_____

_____

Goals

_____

_____

_____

_____

_____

Appointments

_____

_____

Call / Email

_____

_____

Meal Planner

_____

_____

Water Intake

○ ○ ○ ○
○ ○ ○ ○

Steps _____

Notes

"The fact is that given the challenges we face; education doesn't need to be reformed - it needs to be transformed. The key to this transformation is not to standardize education, but to personalize it, to build achievement on discovering the individual talents of each child, to put students in an environment where they want to learn and where they can naturally discover their true passions."
Ken Robinson.

_____

_____

_____

Daily Planner

Date: _____

To do

Morning _____
_____
_____
_____
_____
_____
_____

Afternoon _____
_____
_____
_____
_____
_____
_____

Evening _____
_____
_____
_____
_____
_____
_____

Goals

_____
_____
_____
_____
_____

Appointments

_____
_____

Call / Email

_____
_____

Meal Planner

_____
_____
_____

Water Intake

○ ○ ○
○ ○ ○

Steps _____

Notes

Education is our passport to the future, for tomorrow belongs to the people who prepare for it today. Malcolm X

_____
_____
_____
_____
_____
_____
_____

Date: _____

To do

Morning _____

_____

_____

_____

_____

_____

_____

_____

Afternoon _____

_____

_____

_____

_____

_____

_____

Evening _____

_____

_____

_____

_____

_____

_____

Goals

_____

_____

_____

_____

Appointments

_____

_____

Call / Email

_____

_____

Meal Planner

_____

_____

Water Intake

○ ○ ○ ○
○ ○ ○ ○

Steps _____

Notes

Prejudices, it is well known, are most difficult to
eradicate from the heart whose soil has never been
loosened or fertilized by education: they grow
there, firm as weeds among stones.
Charlotte Bronte

_____

_____

_____

_____

_____

Daily Planner

Date: _____

To do

Morning _____

_____

_____

_____

_____

_____

_____

_____

Afternoon _____

_____

_____

_____

_____

_____

_____

_____

Evening _____

_____

_____

_____

_____

_____

_____

Goals

_____

_____

_____

_____

_____

Appointments

_____

_____

Call / Email

_____

_____

Meal Planner

_____

_____

Water Intake

○ ○ ○ ○
○ ○ ○ ○

Steps _____

Notes

Education without values, as useful as it is, seems rather to make man a more clever devil. C.S. Lewis

_____

_____

_____

_____

_____

_____

Daily Planner

Date: _____

To do

Morning _____

_____

_____

_____

_____

_____

_____

_____

Afternoon _____

_____

_____

_____

_____

_____

_____

Evening _____

_____

_____

_____

_____

_____

Goals

_____

_____

_____

_____

_____

Appointments

_____

_____

Call / Email

_____

_____

Meal Planner

_____

_____

Water Intake

◯ ◯ ◯ ◯
◯ ◯ ◯ ◯

Steps _____

Notes

**The educated differ from the uneducated as much
as the living differ from the dead. Aristotle**

_____

_____

_____

_____

_____

_____

_____

Daily Planner

Date: _____

To do

Morning _____

_____

_____

_____

_____

_____

_____

_____

Afternoon _____

_____

_____

_____

_____

_____

_____

Evening _____

_____

_____

_____

_____

_____

_____

Goals

_____

_____

_____

_____

_____

_____

Appointments

_____

_____

Call / Email

_____

_____

Meal Planner

_____

_____

_____

Water Intake

◯ ◯ ◯ ◯
◯ ◯ ◯ ◯

Steps _____

Notes

Anyone who stops learning is old, whether at twenty or eighty. Anyone who keeps learning stays young. Henry Ford

_____

_____

_____

_____

_____

_____

_____

workout log

Week

Date: _____ Time: _____ Week: _____

Workout Day: ① ② ③ ④ ⑤ ⑥ ⑦

Exercise	Reps	Set -1	Set -2	Set -3	Set -4	Set -5

Date: _____ Time: _____ Week: _____

Workout Day: ① ② ③ ④ ⑤ ⑥ ⑦

Exercise	Reps	Set -1	Set -2	Set -3	Set -4	Set -5

Weight

Body Fat

Chest

Right Arm

Left Arm

Waist

Hips

Right Leg

Left Leg

To Do List This Week

Day _____

Date & Month _____

No.	To Do	Yes/No
_____	_____	☐ ☐
_____	_____	☐ ☐
_____	_____	☐ ☐
_____	_____	☐ ☐
_____	_____	☐ ☐
_____	_____	☐ ☐
_____	_____	☐ ☐
_____	_____	☐ ☐
_____	_____	☐ ☐
_____	_____	☐ ☐
_____	_____	☐ ☐
_____	_____	☐ ☐
_____	_____	☐ ☐
_____	_____	☐ ☐
_____	_____	☐ ☐
_____	_____	☐ ☐
_____	_____	☐ ☐
_____	_____	☐ ☐
_____	_____	☐ ☐
_____	_____	☐ ☐

Notes _____

_____

_____

_____

Daily Planner

Date: _____

To do

Morning _____

_____

_____

_____

_____

_____

_____

_____

Afternoon _____

_____

_____

_____

_____

_____

_____

Evening _____

_____

_____

_____

_____

_____

_____

Goals

_____

_____

_____

_____

_____

Appointments

_____

_____

Call / Email

_____

_____

Meal Planner

_____

_____

Water Intake

◯ ◯ ◯ ◯
◯ ◯ ◯ ◯

Steps _____

Notes

The more I live, the more I learn. The more I learn,
the more I realize, the less I know. Michel Legrand

_____

_____

_____

_____

_____

_____

_____

Daily Planner

Date: _____

To do

Morning _____
_____
_____
_____
_____
_____
_____
_____
_____

Afternoon _____
_____
_____
_____
_____
_____
_____
_____

Evening _____
_____
_____
_____
_____
_____
_____
_____

Goals
_____
_____
_____
_____
_____
_____

Appointments
_____
_____
_____

Call / Email
_____
_____
_____

Meal Planner
_____
_____

Water Intake
◯ ◯ ◯ ◯
◯ ◯ ◯ ◯

Steps _____

Notes

Think the big mistake in schools is trying to teach children anything, and by using fear as the basic motivation. Fear of getting failing grades, fear of not staying with your class, etc. Interest can produce learning on a scale compared to fear as a nuclear explosion to a firecracker. Stanley Kubrick

_____
_____
_____
_____
_____

Daily Planner

Date: _____

To do

Morning _____

_____

_____

_____

_____

_____

_____

_____

Afternoon _____

_____

_____

_____

_____

_____

_____

_____

Evening _____

_____

_____

_____

_____

_____

_____

Goals

_____

_____

_____

_____

_____

Appointments

_____

_____

Call / Email

_____

_____

Meal Planner

_____

_____

Water Intake

◯ ◯ ◯ ◯
◯ ◯ ◯ ◯

Steps _____

Notes

I go to school, but I never learn what I want to know.
Bill Watterson

_____

_____

_____

_____

_____

_____

_____

Daily Planner

Date: _____

To do

Morning _____
_____
_____
_____
_____
_____
_____
_____

Afternoon _____
_____
_____
_____
_____
_____
_____

Evening _____
_____
_____
_____
_____
_____
_____

Goals

_____
_____
_____
_____
_____

Appointments

_____
_____

Call / Email

_____
_____

Meal Planner

_____
_____

Water Intake

◯ ◯ ◯ ◯
◯ ◯ ◯ ◯

Steps _____

Notes

"We will all, at some point, encounter hurdles to gaining access and entry, moving up and conquering self-doubt; but on the other side is the capacity to own opportunity and tell our own story." – Stacey Abrams

_____
_____
_____
_____
_____
_____

Daily Planner

Date: _____

To do

Morning _____

_____

_____

_____

_____

_____

_____

_____

_____

Afternoon _____

_____

_____

_____

_____

_____

_____

Evening _____

_____

_____

_____

_____

_____

_____

Goals

_____

_____

_____

_____

_____

Appointments

_____

_____

Call / Email

_____

_____

Meal Planner

_____

_____

Water Intake

◯ ◯ ◯ ◯
◯ ◯ ◯ ◯

Steps _____

Notes

"If you have no confidence in self, you are twice defeated in the race of life." – Marcus Garvey

_____

_____

_____

_____

_____

_____

_____

Daily Planner

Date: _____

To do

Morning _____

_____

_____

_____

_____

_____

_____

_____

Afternoon _____

_____

_____

_____

_____

_____

_____

Evening _____

_____

_____

_____

_____

_____

_____

Goals

_____

_____

_____

_____

_____

Appointments

_____

_____

_____

Call / Email

_____

_____

_____

Meal Planner

_____

_____

Water Intake

◯ ◯ ◯ ◯
◯ ◯ ◯ ◯

Steps _____

Notes

"I am lucky that whatever fear I have inside me, my desire to win is always stronger." - Serena Williams

_____

_____

_____

_____

_____

_____

Date: _____

To do

Morning _____

_____

_____

_____

_____

_____

_____

_____

_____

Afternoon _____

_____

_____

_____

_____

_____

_____

_____

Evening _____

_____

_____

_____

_____

_____

_____

Goals

_____

_____

_____

_____

_____

Appointments

_____

_____

_____

Call / Email

_____

_____

Meal Planner

_____

_____

Water Intake

◯ ◯ ◯ ◯
◯ ◯ ◯ ◯

Steps _____

Notes

"If they don't give you a seat at the table, bring a folding chair." – Shirley Chisholm

_____

_____

_____

_____

_____

_____

_____

workout log

Week

Date: _____ Time: _____ Week: _____

Workout Day: ① ② ③ ④ ⑤ ⑥ ⑦

Exercise	Reps	Set -1	Set -2	Set -3	Set -4	Set -5

Date: _____ Time: _____ Week: _____

Workout Day: ① ② ③ ④ ⑤ ⑥ ⑦

Exercise	Reps	Set -1	Set -2	Set -3	Set -4	Set -5

Weight

Body Fat

Chest

Right Arm

Left Arm

Waist

Hips

Right Leg

Left Leg

To Do List This Week

Day ——————

Date & Month ——————

No.	To Do	Yes/No	
——	————————————	☐	☐
——	————————————	☐	☐
——	————————————	☐	☐
——	————————————	☐	☐
——	————————————	☐	☐
——	————————————	☐	☐
——	————————————	☐	☐
——	————————————	☐	☐
——	————————————	☐	☐
——	————————————	☐	☐
——	————————————	☐	☐
——	————————————	☐	☐
——	————————————	☐	☐
——	————————————	☐	☐
——	————————————	☐	☐
——	————————————	☐	☐
——	————————————	☐	☐
——	————————————	☐	☐
——	————————————	☐	☐
——	————————————	☐	☐

Notes ————————————————

————————————————————

————————————————————

————————————————————

Daily Planner

Date: _____

To do

Morning _____

_____

_____

_____

_____

_____

_____

_____

Afternoon _____

_____

_____

_____

_____

_____

_____

_____

Evening _____

_____

_____

_____

_____

_____

_____

_____

Goals

_____

_____

_____

_____

_____

Appointments

_____

_____

Call / Email

_____

_____

Meal Planner

_____

_____

_____

Water Intake

○ ○ ○ ○

○ ○ ○ ○

Steps _____

Notes

"The impatient idealist says: 'Give me a place to stand and I shall move the earth.' But such a place does not exist. We all have to stand on the earth itself and go with her at her pace." - Chinua Achebe

_____

_____

_____

_____

_____

_____

Daily Planner

Date: _____

To do

Morning _____
_____
_____
_____
_____
_____
_____
_____

Afternoon _____
_____
_____
_____
_____
_____
_____

Evening _____
_____
_____
_____
_____
_____

Goals
_____
_____
_____
_____
_____

Appointments
_____
_____

Call / Email
_____
_____

Meal Planner
_____
_____

Water Intake
◯ ◯ ◯ ◯
◯ ◯ ◯ ◯

Steps _____

Notes
"The most common way people give up their power is by thinking they don't have any." - Alice Walker
_____
_____
_____
_____
_____
_____
_____

Date: _____

To do

Morning _____

_____

_____

_____

_____

_____

_____

_____

Afternoon _____

_____

_____

_____

_____

_____

_____

_____

Evening _____

_____

_____

_____

_____

_____

_____

Goals

_____

_____

_____

_____

_____

Appointments

_____

_____

_____

Call / Email

_____

_____

Meal Planner

_____

_____

Water Intake

○ ○ ○ ○
○ ○ ○ ○

Steps _____

Notes

"Every time you state what you want or believe, you're the first to hear it. It's a message to both you and others about what you think is possible. Don't put a ceiling on yourself." – Oprah Winfrey

_____

_____

_____

_____

_____

_____

Daily Planner

Date: _____

To do

Morning _____

_____

_____

_____

_____

_____

_____

Afternoon _____

_____

_____

_____

_____

_____

_____

Evening _____

_____

_____

_____

_____

_____

Goals

_____

_____

_____

_____

_____

Appointments

_____

_____

Call / Email

_____

_____

Meal Planner

_____

_____

Water Intake

◯ ◯ ◯ ◯

◯ ◯ ◯ ◯

Steps _____

Notes

"Freeing yourself was one thing; claiming ownership of that freed self was another."
Toni Morrison

_____

_____

_____

_____

_____

_____

_____

_____

Daily Planner

Date: _____

To do

Morning _____

_____

_____

_____

_____

_____

_____

_____

Afternoon _____

_____

_____

_____

_____

_____

_____

Evening _____

_____

_____

_____

_____

_____

_____

Goals

_____

_____

_____

_____

_____

Appointments

_____

_____

Call / Email

_____

_____

Meal Planner

_____

_____

Water Intake

◯ ◯ ◯ ◯
◯ ◯ ◯ ◯

Steps _____

Notes

"Every great dream begins with a dreamer. Always remember, you have within you the strength, the patience, and the passion to reach for the stars to change the world." – Harriet Tubman

_____

_____

_____

_____

_____

_____

_____

Daily Planner

Date: _____

To do

Morning _____

_____

_____

_____

_____

_____

_____

_____

Afternoon _____

_____

_____

_____

_____

_____

_____

Evening _____

_____

_____

_____

_____

_____

_____

Goals

_____

_____

_____

_____

_____

Appointments

_____

_____

Call / Email

_____

_____

Meal Planner

_____

_____

Water Intake

◯ ◯ ◯ ◯
◯ ◯ ◯ ◯

Steps _____

Notes

"I will not take 'but' for an answer." – Langston Hughes

_____

_____

_____

_____

_____

_____

Daily Planner

Date: _____

To do

Morning _____

_____

_____

_____

_____

_____

_____

_____

Afternoon _____

_____

_____

_____

_____

_____

_____

_____

Evening _____

_____

_____

_____

_____

_____

_____

Goals

_____

_____

_____

_____

_____

Appointments

_____

_____

_____

Call / Email

_____

_____

_____

Meal Planner

_____

_____

_____

Water Intake

◯ ◯ ◯
◯ ◯ ◯

Steps _____

Notes

"When I dare to be powerful, to use my strength in the service of my vision, then it becomes less and less important whether I am afraid." – Audre Lorde

_____

_____

_____

_____

_____

_____

_____

MY MEETING NOTES

MEETING NAME & DATE -

ATTENDEES -

NEXT STEPS / DEADLINES -

MEETING NOTES -

"Never be limited by other people's limited imaginations." - Dr. Mae Jemison

MY MEETING NOTES

MEETING NAME & DATE -

ATTENDEES -

NEXT STEPS / DEADLINES -

MEETING NOTES -

"The soul that is within me no man can degrade." - Frederick Douglass

MY MEETING NOTES

MEETING NAME & DATE -

ATTENDEES -

NEXT STEPS / DEADLINES -

MEETING NOTES -

"We will all, at some point, encounter hurdles to gaining access and entry, moving up and conquering self-doubt; but on the other side is the capacity to own opportunity and tell our own story." – Stacey Abrams

MY MEETING NOTES

MEETING NAME & DATE -

ATTENDEES -

NEXT STEPS / DEADLINES -

MEETING NOTES -

"If you have no confidence in self, you are twice defeated in the race of life." - Marcus Garvey

MY MEETING NOTES

MEETING NAME & DATE -

ATTENDEES -

NEXT STEPS / DEADLINES -

MEETING NOTES -

_____
_____
_____
_____
_____
_____
_____
_____
_____
_____
_____
_____
_____
_____
_____
_____
_____
_____
_____

"I am lucky that whatever fear I have inside me, my desire to win is always stronger."
Serena Williams

MY MEETING NOTES

MEETING NAME & DATE -

ATTENDEES -

NEXT STEPS / DEADLINES -

MEETING NOTES -

_____

_____

_____

_____

_____

_____

_____

_____

_____

_____

_____

_____

_____

_____

_____

_____

_____

_____

_____

"If they don't give you a seat at the table, bring a folding chair." – Shirley Chisholm

MY MEETING NOTES

MEETING NAME & DATE -

ATTENDEES -

NEXT STEPS / DEADLINES -

MEETING NOTES -

"The impatient idealist says: 'Give me a place to stand and I shall move the earth.' But such a place does not exist. We all have to stand on the earth itself and go with her at her pace."
Chinua Achebe

MY MEETING NOTES

MEETING NAME & DATE -

ATTENDEES -

NEXT STEPS / DEADLINES -

MEETING NOTES -

"The most common way people give up their power is by thinking they don't have any."
Alice Walker

MY MEETING NOTES

MEETING NAME & DATE -

ATTENDEES -

NEXT STEPS / DEADLINES -

MEETING NOTES -

_____

_____

_____

_____

_____

_____

_____

_____

_____

_____

_____

_____

_____

_____

_____

_____

_____

_____

"Every time you state what you want or believe, you're the first to hear it. It's a message to both you and others about what you think is possible. Don't put a ceiling on yourself."
Oprah Winfrey

MY MEETING NOTES

MEETING NAME & DATE -

ATTENDEES -

NEXT STEPS / DEADLINES -

MEETING NOTES -

_____
_____
_____
_____
_____
_____
_____
_____
_____
_____
_____
_____
_____
_____
_____
_____
_____
_____

"Freeing yourself was one thing; claiming ownership of that freed self was another." –
Toni Morrison

MY MEETING NOTES

MEETING NAME & DATE -

ATTENDEES -

NEXT STEPS / DEADLINES -

MEETING NOTES -

"Every great dream begins with a dreamer. Always remember, you have within you the strength, the patience, and the passion to reach for the stars to change the world."
Harriet Tubman

MY MEETING NOTES

MEETING NAME & DATE -

ATTENDEES -

NEXT STEPS / DEADLINES -

MEETING NOTES -

"I really don't think life is about the I-could-have-beens. Life is only about the I-tried-to-do. I don't mind the failure, but I can't imagine that I'd forgive myself if I didn't try." —Nikki Giovanni

MONTHLY REVIEW

THIS MONTH I ACHIEVED

_____

_____

_____

_____

_____

_____

_____

_____

WHAT WORKED

_____

_____

_____

_____

WHAT DIDN'T WORK

_____

_____

_____

_____

DO MORE OF

DO LESS OF

MONTHLY REVIEW

MONTH OF

THIS MONTH I ACHIEVED

_____

_____

_____

_____

_____

_____

_____

_____

_____

WHAT WORKED

_____

_____

_____

WHAT DIDN'T WORK

_____

_____

_____

DO MORE OF	DO LESS OF

JUNE

YOUR FITNESS SAMPLE

MON
LEGS

Stretching and warm-up
25 Squats
25 Sumo Squats
Repeat above March in place for 20 sec
Stretch muscles
Relax

TUES
ABS

Stretching and warm-up
20 Standing Oblique Twists
30-second Floor Plank
Repeat above
March in place for 20 seconds
Stretch muscles
Relax

WED
ARMS

Stretching and warm-up
25 Push-ups
20 Wall Tricep Pushes
Repeat above
March in place for 20 seconds
Stretch muscles
Relax

THURS
CARDIO

Stretching and warm-up
50 Jumping Jacks
30-second Sprint in place
Repeat above
March in place for 20 seconds
Stretch muscles
Relax

FRI
COMBO

Stretching and warm-up
10 Squats & 10 Sumo Squats
10 Standing Oblique Twists
March in place for 20 seconds
20 Push-ups
25 Jumping Jacks
March in place for 20 seconds
Stretch muscles
Relax

SAT
YOUR PICK

Choose from Day 1-4
to work on your chosen area:
Legs
Abs
Arms or
Cardio

SUN
REST

Take a break!
You deserve it.

workout log

Week

Date: Time: Week:

Workout Day: ①   ②   ③   ④   ⑤   ⑥   ⑦

Exercise	Reps	Set -1	Set -2	Set -3	Set -4	Set -5

Date: Time: Week:

Workout Day: ①   ②   ③   ④   ⑤   ⑥   ⑦

Exercise	Reps	Set -1	Set -2	Set -3	Set -4	Set -5

Weight

Body Fat

Chest

Right Arm

Left Arm

Waist

Hips

Right Leg

Left Leg

THIS MONTH'S LIST

Month: June Year: _____

Potential Items to Plan/Schedule:

District Board Mtg
District Principal Mtg
Campus Admin Mtg
Vertical Team Mtg
Parent Conferences
LPACs/ELLs/ARDs
Progress Reports/Report Cards
Master Schedule Review
Team Leader/Dept. Chair Mtg
Professional Learning Community (PLC) Mtg
Athletic Event Admin Coverage Schedule
Teachers I need to meet with (observe/walkthrough)

Potential Assessments

Campus Level Assessments-State Aligned Objectives

Additions

Shared Decision Making Council (SDMC)
Graduation Planning Review
Summer School Preparation & Planning
Promotion/Retention Conferences w/Parents
State Testing Planning & Roster Development

_____

_____

_____

_____

_____

_____

_____

MONTHLY PLANNER
MONTH: _____

MONDAY	TUESDAY	WEDNESDAY	THURSDAY	FRIDAY	SATURDAY	SUNDAY

PRIORITY

To Do List This Week

Day _____

Date & Month _____

No.	To Do	Yes/No
_____	_____	☐ ☐
_____	_____	☐ ☐
_____	_____	☐ ☐
_____	_____	☐ ☐
_____	_____	☐ ☐
_____	_____	☐ ☐
_____	_____	☐ ☐
_____	_____	☐ ☐
_____	_____	☐ ☐
_____	_____	☐ ☐
_____	_____	☐ ☐
_____	_____	☐ ☐
_____	_____	☐ ☐
_____	_____	☐ ☐
_____	_____	☐ ☐
_____	_____	☐ ☐
_____	_____	☐ ☐
_____	_____	☐ ☐
_____	_____	☐ ☐
_____	_____	☐ ☐

Notes _____

_____

_____

_____

Date: _____

To do

Morning _____

_____
_____
_____
_____
_____
_____
_____

Afternoon _____

_____
_____
_____
_____
_____
_____

Evening _____

_____
_____
_____
_____
_____
_____
_____

Goals

_____
_____
_____
_____
_____

Appointments

_____
_____
_____

Call / Email

_____
_____
_____

Meal Planner

_____
_____

Water Intake

◯ ◯ ◯ ◯
◯ ◯ ◯ ◯

Steps _____

Notes

To educate a person in the mind but not in morals is to educate a menace to society. Theodore Roosevelt

_____
_____
_____
_____
_____
_____
_____

Daily Planner

Date: _____

To do

Morning _____

_____

_____

_____

_____

_____

_____

_____

Afternoon _____

_____

_____

_____

_____

_____

_____

Evening _____

_____

_____

_____

_____

_____

_____

Goals

_____

_____

_____

_____

_____

Appointments

_____

_____

_____

Call / Email

_____

_____

_____

Meal Planner

_____

_____

Water Intake

◯ ◯ ◯ ◯
◯ ◯ ◯ ◯

Steps _____

Notes

Formal education will make you a living; self-education will make you a fortune. Jim Rohn

_____

_____

_____

_____

_____

_____

_____

Date: _____

To do

Morning _____

_____

_____

_____

_____

_____

_____

_____

Afternoon _____

_____

_____

_____

_____

_____

_____

Evening _____

_____

_____

_____

_____

_____

_____

Goals

_____

_____

_____

_____

Appointments

_____

_____

Call / Email

_____

_____

Meal Planner

_____

_____

Water Intake

◯ ◯ ◯ ◯
◯ ◯ ◯ ◯

Steps _____

Notes

We spend the first year of a child's life teaching it to walk and talk and the rest of its life to shut up and sit down. There's something wrong there.
Neil deGrasse Tyson

_____

_____

_____

_____

_____

_____

_____

Daily Planner

Date: _____

To do

Morning _____
_____
_____
_____
_____
_____
_____
_____

Afternoon _____
_____
_____
_____
_____
_____
_____

Evening _____
_____
_____
_____
_____
_____
_____

Goals
_____
_____
_____
_____
_____

Appointments
_____
_____

Call / Email
_____
_____

Meal Planner
_____
_____

Water Intake
○ ○ ○ ○
○ ○ ○ ○

Steps _____

Notes
Do you know the difference between education and experience? Education is when you read the fine print; experience is what you get when you don't.
Pete Seeger
_____
_____
_____
_____
_____
_____
_____

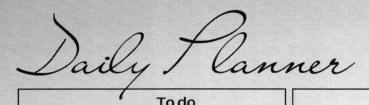

Date: _____

To do

Morning _____

_____

_____

_____

_____

_____

_____

_____

Afternoon _____

_____

_____

_____

_____

_____

_____

Evening _____

_____

_____

_____

_____

_____

_____

Goals

_____

_____

_____

_____

_____

Appointments

_____

_____

Call / Email

_____

_____

Meal Planner

_____

_____

Water Intake

◯ ◯ ◯ ◯
◯ ◯ ◯ ◯

Steps _____

Notes

True teachers are those who use themselves as bridges over which they invite their students to cross; then, having facilitated their crossing, joyfully collapse, encouraging them to create their own. Nikos Kazantzakis

_____

_____

_____

_____

_____

_____

Daily Planner

Date: _____

To do

Morning _____

_____

_____

_____

_____

_____

_____

_____

Afternoon _____

_____

_____

_____

_____

_____

_____

Evening _____

_____

_____

_____

_____

_____

_____

Goals

_____

_____

_____

_____

_____

Appointments

_____

_____

_____

Call / Email

_____

_____

_____

Meal Planner

_____

_____

Water Intake

◯ ◯ ◯ ◯
◯ ◯ ◯ ◯

Steps _____

Notes

Wisdom.... comes not from age, but from education and learning. Anton Chekhov

_____

_____

_____

_____

_____

_____

_____

Daily Planner

Date: _____

To do

Morning _____

_____

_____

_____

_____

_____

_____

Afternoon _____

_____

_____

_____

_____

_____

_____

Evening _____

_____

_____

_____

_____

_____

_____

Goals

_____

_____

_____

_____

_____

Appointments

_____

_____

Call / Email

_____

_____

Meal Planner

_____

_____

Water Intake

○ ○ ○ ○
○ ○ ○ ○

Steps _____

Notes

"Integrating technology with face-to-face teacher time generally produces better academic outcomes than employing either technique alone."

_____

_____

_____

_____

_____

_____

_____

_____

workout log

Week

Date : _____   Time : _____   Week : _____

Workout Day : ① ② ③ ④ ⑤ ⑥ ⑦

Exercise	Reps	Set -1	Set -2	Set -3	Set -4	Set -5

Date : _____   Time : _____   Week : _____

Workout Day : ① ② ③ ④ ⑤ ⑥ ⑦

Exercise	Reps	Set -1	Set -2	Set -3	Set -4	Set -5

Weight

Body Fat

Chest

Right Arm

Left Arm

Waist

Hips

Right Leg

Left Leg

To Do List This Week

Day _____

Date & Month _____

No.	To Do	Yes/No
_____	_____	☐ ☐
_____	_____	☐ ☐
_____	_____	☐ ☐
_____	_____	☐ ☐
_____	_____	☐ ☐
_____	_____	☐ ☐
_____	_____	☐ ☐
_____	_____	☐ ☐
_____	_____	☐ ☐
_____	_____	☐ ☐
_____	_____	☐ ☐
_____	_____	☐ ☐
_____	_____	☐ ☐
_____	_____	☐ ☐
_____	_____	☐ ☐
_____	_____	☐ ☐
_____	_____	☐ ☐
_____	_____	☐ ☐
_____	_____	☐ ☐
_____	_____	☐ ☐

Notes _____

_____

_____

_____

Daily Planner

Date: _____

To do

Morning _____

_____

_____

_____

_____

_____

_____

_____

Afternoon _____

_____

_____

_____

_____

_____

_____

Evening _____

_____

_____

_____

_____

_____

Goals

_____

_____

_____

_____

Appointments

_____

_____

Call / Email

_____

_____

Meal Planner

_____

_____

Water Intake

○ ○ ○ ○
○ ○ ○ ○

Steps _____

Notes

I would rather entertain and hope that people learned something than educate people and hope they were entertained. Walt Disney Company

_____

_____

_____

_____

_____

_____

_____

Daily Planner

Date: _____

To do

Morning _____
_____
_____
_____
_____
_____
_____
_____

Afternoon _____
_____
_____
_____
_____
_____
_____

Evening _____
_____
_____
_____
_____
_____
_____

Goals

_____
_____
_____
_____

Appointments

_____
_____

Call / Email

_____
_____

Meal Planner

_____
_____

Water Intake

◯ ◯ ◯ ◯
◯ ◯ ◯ ◯

Steps _____

Notes

Education is the power to think clearly, the power to act well in the world's work, and the power to appreciate life. Brigham Young

_____
_____
_____
_____
_____
_____

Daily Planner

Date: _____

To do

Morning _____

_____
_____
_____
_____
_____
_____
_____

Afternoon _____

_____
_____
_____
_____
_____
_____
_____

Evening _____

_____
_____
_____
_____
_____
_____
_____

Goals

_____
_____
_____
_____
_____

Appointments

_____
_____

Call / Email

_____
_____

Meal Planner

_____
_____

Water Intake

◯ ◯ ◯
◯ ◯ ◯

Steps _____

Notes

When you take the free will out of education, that turns it into schooling. John Taylor Gatto

_____
_____
_____
_____
_____
_____

Date: _____

To do

Morning _____

_____

_____

_____

_____

_____

_____

_____

Afternoon _____

_____

_____

_____

_____

_____

_____

Evening _____

_____

_____

_____

_____

_____

_____

Goals

_____

_____

_____

_____

_____

Appointments

_____

_____

Call / Email

_____

_____

Meal Planner

_____

_____

Water Intake

○ ○ ○
○ ○ ○

Steps _____

Notes

Where there is no vision, the people perish. — Proverbs 29:18

_____

_____

_____

_____

_____

_____

_____

_____

Daily Planner

Date: _____

To do

Morning _____
_____
_____
_____
_____
_____
_____
_____

Afternoon _____
_____
_____
_____
_____
_____
_____
_____

Evening _____
_____
_____
_____
_____
_____
_____
_____

Goals
_____
_____
_____
_____
_____
_____

Appointments
_____
_____
_____

Call / Email
_____
_____
_____

Meal Planner
_____
_____

Water Intake
○ ○ ○ ○
○ ○ ○ ○

Steps _____

Notes

To command is to serve, nothing more and nothing less. —Andre Malraux

_____
_____
_____
_____
_____
_____
_____

Daily Planner

Date: _____

To do

Morning _____

_____

_____

_____

_____

_____

_____

_____

Afternoon _____

_____

_____

_____

_____

_____

_____

Evening _____

_____

_____

_____

_____

_____

_____

Goals

_____

_____

_____

_____

Appointments

_____

_____

Call / Email

_____

_____

Meal Planner

_____

_____

Water Intake

○ ○ ○ ○
○ ○ ○ ○

Steps _____

Notes

Become the kind of leader that people would follow voluntarily, even if you had no title or position. —Brian Tracy

_____

_____

_____

_____

_____

_____

_____

Daily Planner

Date: _____

To do

Morning _____
_____
_____
_____
_____
_____
_____
_____

Afternoon _____
_____
_____
_____
_____
_____
_____

Evening _____
_____
_____
_____
_____
_____
_____

Goals

_____
_____
_____
_____
_____
_____

Appointments

_____
_____
_____

Call / Email

_____
_____

Meal Planner

_____
_____

Water Intake

◯ ◯ ◯ ◯
◯ ◯ ◯ ◯

Steps _____

Notes

I start with the premise that the function of leadership is to produce more leaders, not more followers. —Ralph Nader

_____
_____
_____
_____
_____
_____
_____

workout log

Week

Date: _____ Time: _____ Week: _____

Weight

Workout Day: ① ② ③ ④ ⑤ ⑥ ⑦

Exercise	Reps	Set -1	Set -2	Set -3	Set -4	Set -5

Body Fat

Chest

Right Arm

Left Arm

Date: _____ Time: _____ Week: _____

Waist

Workout Day: ① ② ③ ④ ⑤ ⑥ ⑦

Exercise	Reps	Set -1	Set -2	Set -3	Set -4	Set -5

Hips

Right Leg

Left Leg

To Do List This Week

Day _____

Date & Month _____

No.	To Do	Yes/No
		☐ ☐
		☐ ☐
		☐ ☐
		☐ ☐
		☐ ☐
		☐ ☐
		☐ ☐
		☐ ☐
		☐ ☐
		☐ ☐
		☐ ☐
		☐ ☐
		☐ ☐
		☐ ☐
		☐ ☐
		☐ ☐
		☐ ☐
		☐ ☐
		☐ ☐
		☐ ☐

Notes _____

_____

_____

_____

Daily Planner

Date: _____

To do

Morning _____
_____
_____
_____
_____
_____
_____
_____
_____

Afternoon _____
_____
_____
_____
_____
_____
_____
_____

Evening _____
_____
_____
_____
_____
_____
_____
_____

Goals
_____
_____
_____
_____
_____

Appointments
_____
_____

Call / Email
_____
_____

Meal Planner
_____
_____

Water Intake
◯ ◯ ◯ ◯
◯ ◯ ◯ ◯

Steps _____

Notes
Effective leadership is not about making speeches or being liked; leadership is defined by results not attributes. —Peter Drucker
_____
_____
_____
_____
_____
_____
_____
_____

Daily Planner

Date: _____

To do

Morning _____

_____

_____

_____

_____

_____

_____

_____

Afternoon _____

_____

_____

_____

_____

_____

_____

Evening _____

_____

_____

_____

_____

_____

Goals

_____

_____

_____

_____

Appointments

_____

_____

Call / Email

_____

_____

Meal Planner

_____

_____

Water Intake

◯ ◯ ◯ ◯
◯ ◯ ◯ ◯

Steps _____

Notes

The best executive is the one who has sense enough to pick good men to do what he wants done, and self-restraint enough to keep from meddling with them while they do it. —Theodore Roosevelt

_____

_____

_____

_____

_____

_____

Daily Planner

Date: _____

To do

Morning _____

_____

_____

_____

_____

_____

_____

_____

Afternoon _____

_____

_____

_____

_____

_____

_____

_____

Evening _____

_____

_____

_____

_____

_____

_____

Goals

_____

_____

_____

_____

_____

Appointments

_____

_____

_____

Call / Email

_____

_____

_____

Meal Planner

_____

_____

Water Intake

◯ ◯ ◯ ◯
◯ ◯ ◯ ◯

Steps _____

Notes

Leadership is influence. —John C. Maxwell

_____

_____

_____

_____

_____

_____

_____

Daily Planner

Date: _____

To do

Morning _____
_____
_____
_____
_____
_____
_____
_____

Afternoon _____
_____
_____
_____
_____
_____
_____
_____

Evening _____
_____
_____
_____
_____
_____
_____

Goals
_____
_____
_____
_____
_____

Appointments
_____
_____

Call / Email
_____
_____

Meal Planner
_____
_____

Water Intake
◯ ◯ ◯ ◯
◯ ◯ ◯ ◯

Steps _____

Notes

When I give a minister an order, I leave it to him to find the means to carry it out.
Napoleon Bonaparte
_____
_____
_____
_____
_____
_____
_____

Daily Planner

Date: _____

To do

Morning _____

_____

_____

_____

_____

_____

_____

_____

Afternoon _____

_____

_____

_____

_____

_____

_____

Evening _____

_____

_____

_____

_____

_____

_____

Goals

_____

_____

_____

_____

Appointments

_____

_____

Call / Email

_____

_____

Meal Planner

_____

_____

Water Intake

◯ ◯ ◯ ◯
◯ ◯ ◯ ◯

Steps _____

Notes

Men make history and not the other way around. In periods where there is no leadership, society stands still. Progress occurs when courageous, skillful leaders seize the opportunity to change things for the better. —Harry S. Truman

_____

_____

_____

_____

_____

_____

Daily Planner

Date: _____

To do

Morning _____
_____
_____
_____
_____
_____
_____
_____

Afternoon _____
_____
_____
_____
_____
_____
_____

Evening _____
_____
_____
_____
_____
_____
_____

Goals

_____
_____
_____
_____
_____

Appointments

_____
_____
_____

Call / Email

_____
_____
_____

Meal Planner

_____
_____

Water Intake

◯ ◯ ◯ ◯
◯ ◯ ◯ ◯

Steps _____

Notes

The key to successful leadership today is influence, not authority. —Kenneth Blanchard

_____
_____
_____
_____
_____
_____
_____

Daily Planner

Date: _____

To do

Morning _____

_____

_____

_____

_____

_____

_____

_____

Afternoon _____

_____

_____

_____

_____

_____

_____

_____

Evening _____

_____

_____

_____

_____

_____

_____

Goals

_____

_____

_____

_____

Appointments

_____

_____

Call / Email

_____

_____

Meal Planner

_____

_____

Water Intake

◯ ◯ ◯ ◯
◯ ◯ ◯ ◯

Steps _____

Notes

A leader takes people where they want to go. A great leader takes people where they don't necessarily want to go, but ought to be. —Rosalynn Carter

_____

_____

_____

_____

_____

_____

_____

workout log

Week

Date: _____ Time: _____ Week: _____

Weight

Workout Day: ① ② ③ ④ ⑤ ⑥ ⑦

Body Fat

Exercise	Reps	Set -1	Set -2	Set -3	Set -4	Set -5

Chest

Right Arm

Left Arm

Date: _____ Time: _____ Week: _____

Waist

Workout Day: ① ② ③ ④ ⑤ ⑥ ⑦

Hips

Exercise	Reps	Set -1	Set -2	Set -3	Set -4	Set -5

Right Leg

Left Leg

To Do List This Week

Day _____

Date & Month _____

No.	To Do	Yes/No
_____	_____	☐ ☐
_____	_____	☐ ☐
_____	_____	☐ ☐
_____	_____	☐ ☐
_____	_____	☐ ☐
_____	_____	☐ ☐
_____	_____	☐ ☐
_____	_____	☐ ☐
_____	_____	☐ ☐
_____	_____	☐ ☐
_____	_____	☐ ☐
_____	_____	☐ ☐
_____	_____	☐ ☐
_____	_____	☐ ☐
_____	_____	☐ ☐
_____	_____	☐ ☐
_____	_____	☐ ☐
_____	_____	☐ ☐
_____	_____	☐ ☐

Notes _____

_____

_____

_____

Daily Planner

Date: _____

To do

Morning _____
_____
_____
_____
_____
_____
_____
_____

Afternoon _____
_____
_____
_____
_____
_____
_____

Evening _____
_____
_____
_____
_____
_____
_____
_____

Goals
_____
_____
_____
_____

Appointments
_____
_____

Call / Email
_____
_____

Meal Planner
_____
_____

Water Intake

Steps _____

Notes

The challenge of leadership is to be strong, but not rude; be kind, but not weak; be bold, but not bully; be thoughtful, but not lazy; be humble, but not timid; be proud, but not arrogant; have humor, but without folly. —Jim Rohn

_____
_____
_____
_____
_____

Daily Planner

Date: _____

To do

Morning _____
_____
_____
_____
_____
_____
_____
_____

Afternoon _____
_____
_____
_____
_____
_____
_____

Evening _____
_____
_____
_____
_____
_____

Goals

_____
_____
_____
_____
_____

Appointments

_____
_____
_____

Call / Email

_____
_____

Meal Planner

_____
_____

Water Intake

○ ○ ○ ○
○ ○ ○ ○

Steps _____

Notes

Outstanding leaders go out of their way to boost the self-esteem of their personnel. If people believe in themselves, it's amazing what they can accomplish.
—Sam Walton

_____
_____
_____
_____
_____
_____
_____

Daily Planner

Date: _____

To do

Morning _____
_____
_____
_____
_____
_____
_____

Afternoon _____
_____
_____
_____
_____
_____
_____
_____

Evening _____
_____
_____
_____
_____
_____
_____

Goals

_____
_____
_____
_____

Appointments

_____
_____

Call / Email

_____
_____

Meal Planner

_____
_____

Water Intake

◯ ◯ ◯ ◯
◯ ◯ ◯ ◯

Steps _____

Notes

A true leader has the confidence to stand alone, the courage to make tough decisions, and the compassion to listen to the needs of others. He does not set out to be a leader, but becomes one by the equality of his actions and the integrity of his intent.
—Douglas MacArthur
_____
_____
_____
_____
_____
_____

Daily Planner

Date: _____

To do

Morning _____
_____
_____
_____
_____
_____
_____
_____

Afternoon _____
_____
_____
_____
_____
_____
_____

Evening _____
_____
_____
_____
_____
_____
_____

Goals

_____
_____
_____
_____
_____

Appointments

_____
_____

Call / Email

_____
_____

Meal Planner

_____
_____

Water Intake

○ ○ ○ ○
○ ○ ○ ○

Steps _____

Notes

As we look ahead into the next century, leaders will be those who empower others. —Bill Gates

_____
_____
_____
_____
_____
_____
_____
_____

Daily Planner

Date: _____

To do

Morning _____
_____
_____
_____
_____
_____
_____
_____

Afternoon _____
_____
_____
_____
_____
_____
_____

Evening _____
_____
_____
_____
_____
_____
_____

Goals
_____
_____
_____
_____
_____

Appointments
_____
_____
_____

Call / Email
_____
_____
_____

Meal Planner
_____
_____

Water Intake

○ ○ ○ ○
○ ○ ○ ○

Steps _____

Notes

All of the great leaders have had one characteristic in common: it was the willingness to confront unequivocally the major anxiety of their people in their time. This, and not much else, is the essence of leadership. —John Kenneth Galbraith

_____
_____
_____
_____
_____
_____
_____

Daily Planner

Date: _____

To do

Morning _____

_____

_____

_____

_____

_____

_____

_____

Afternoon _____

_____

_____

_____

_____

_____

_____

Evening _____

_____

_____

_____

_____

_____

_____

Goals

_____

_____

_____

_____

Appointments

_____

_____

Call / Email

_____

_____

Meal Planner

_____

_____

Water Intake

◯ ◯ ◯ ◯
◯ ◯ ◯ ◯

Steps _____

Notes

Do what you feel in your heart to be right–for you'll
be criticized anyway. —Eleanor Roosevelt

_____

_____

_____

_____

_____

_____

_____

Daily Planner

Date: _____

To do

Morning _____

_____

_____

_____

_____

_____

_____

Afternoon _____

_____

_____

_____

_____

_____

_____

Evening _____

_____

_____

_____

_____

_____

_____

Goals

_____

_____

_____

_____

_____

Appointments

_____

_____

_____

Call / Email

_____

_____

_____

Meal Planner

_____

_____

Water Intake

○ ○ ○ ○
○ ○ ○ ○

Steps _____

Notes

"I was raised to believe that excellence is the best deterrent to racism or sexism. And that's how I operate my life." – Oprah Winfrey

_____

_____

_____

_____

_____

_____

MY MEETING NOTES

MEETING NAME & DATE -

ATTENDEES -

NEXT STEPS / DEADLINES -

MEETING NOTES -

"Almost always, the creative dedicated minority has made the world better."
Martin Luther King, Jr.

MY MEETING NOTES

MEETING NAME & DATE -

ATTENDEES -

NEXT STEPS / DEADLINES -

MEETING NOTES -

"One of the lessons that I grew up with was to always stay true to yourself and never let what somebody else says distract you from your goals. And so when I hear about negative and false attacks, I really don't invest any energy in them, because I know who I am."
Michelle Obama

MY MEETING NOTES

MEETING NAME & DATE -

ATTENDEES -

NEXT STEPS / DEADLINES -

MEETING NOTES -

_____

_____

_____

_____

_____

_____

_____

_____

_____

_____

_____

_____

_____

_____

_____

_____

_____

_____

_____

"I am America. I am the part you won't recognize. But get used to me. Black, confident, cocky;
my name, not yours; my religion, not yours; my goals, my own; get used to me."
Muhammad Ali

MY MEETING NOTES

MEETING NAME & DATE -

ATTENDEES -

NEXT STEPS / DEADLINES -

MEETING NOTES -

"Have a vision of excellence, a dream of success, and work like hell."
Dr. Samuel DuBois Cook

MY MEETING NOTES

MEETING NAME & DATE -

ATTENDEES -

NEXT STEPS / DEADLINES -

MEETING NOTES -

_____

_____

_____

_____

_____

_____

_____

_____

_____

_____

_____

_____

_____

_____

_____

_____

_____

_____

_____

_____

"The very serious function of racism is distraction. It keeps you from doing your work. It keeps you explaining, over and over again, your reason for being." – Toni Morrison

MY MEETING NOTES

MEETING NAME & DATE -

ATTENDEES -

NEXT STEPS / DEADLINES -

MEETING NOTES -

_____
_____
_____
_____
_____
_____
_____
_____
_____
_____
_____
_____
_____
_____
_____
_____
_____
_____
_____

"Those who say it can't be done are usually interrupted by others doing it."
James Baldwin

MY MEETING NOTES

MEETING NAME & DATE -

ATTENDEES -

NEXT STEPS / DEADLINES -

MEETING NOTES -

_____
_____
_____
_____
_____
_____
_____
_____
_____
_____
_____
_____
_____
_____
_____
_____
_____
_____
_____

"To me, we are the most beautiful creatures in the whole world. Black people. And I mean that in every sense." – Nina Simone

MY MEETING NOTES

MEETING NAME & DATE -

ATTENDEES -

NEXT STEPS / DEADLINES -

MEETING NOTES -

"We need to internalize this idea of excellence. Not many folks spend a lot of time trying to be excellent." - Barack Obama

MY MEETING NOTES

MEETING NAME & DATE -

ATTENDEES -

NEXT STEPS / DEADLINES -

MEETING NOTES -

_____

_____

_____

_____

_____

_____

_____

_____

_____

_____

_____

_____

_____

_____

_____

_____

_____

_____

_____

_____

"The things that make us different, those are our super powers." - Lena Waithe

MY MEETING NOTES

MEETING NAME & DATE -

ATTENDEES -

NEXT STEPS / DEADLINES -

MEETING NOTES -

_____
_____
_____
_____
_____
_____
_____
_____
_____
_____
_____
_____
_____
_____
_____
_____
_____
_____
_____
_____

"If you can be the best, then why not try to be the best?" – Garrett Morgan

MY MEETING NOTES

MEETING NAME & DATE -

ATTENDEES -

NEXT STEPS / DEADLINES -

MEETING NOTES -

_____
_____
_____
_____
_____
_____
_____
_____
_____
_____
_____
_____
_____
_____
_____
_____
_____
_____
_____

"Never be limited by other people's limited imaginations." - Dr. Mae Jemison

MY MEETING NOTES

MEETING NAME & DATE -

ATTENDEES -

NEXT STEPS / DEADLINES -

MEETING NOTES -

_____

_____

_____

_____

_____

_____

_____

_____

_____

_____

_____

_____

_____

_____

_____

_____

_____

_____

"The soul that is within me no man can degrade." - Frederick Douglass

MONTHLY REVIEW

MONTH OF

THIS MONTH I ACHIEVED

_____
_____
_____
_____
_____
_____
_____
_____

WHAT WORKED

_____
_____
_____
_____

WHAT DIDN'T WORK

_____
_____
_____
_____

DO MORE OF

DO LESS OF

Yearly Review

YEAR

TOP ACCOMPLISHMENTS

-
-
-
-
-
-

HIGHLIGHTS

SETBACKS

THINGS TO LEARN

THINGS TO CHANGE

START

STOP

CONTINUE

NEXT YEAR PRIORITIES

-
-
-
-
-
-

Yearly Review

YEAR

TOP ACCOMPLISHMENTS

HIGHLIGHTS

SETBACKS

THINGS TO LEARN

THINGS TO CHANGE

START

STOP

CONTINUE

NEXT YEAR PRIORITIES

Made in the USA
Middletown, DE
05 September 2022

72667094R00300